Jesus Sang the Psalms

Learning About God While Singing the Psalms

John M Harris

authorHOUSE™

1663 LIBERTY DRIVE, SUITE 200
BLOOMINGTON, INDIANA 47403
(800) 839-8640
WWW.AUTHORHOUSE.COM

First published by AuthorHouse 07/15/05

ISBN: 1-4208-6103-4 (e)
ISBN: 1-4208-6101-8 (sc)
ISBN: 1-4208-6102-6 (dj)

Library of Congress Control Number: 2005904891

Printed in the United States of America
Bloomington, Indiana

This book is printed on acid-free paper.

DEDICATION

Kenneth D. Shick, D. Min.

Colleague and friend *extraordinarie*

CONTENTS

ACKNOWLEDGEMENTS

It seems to me that for a preacher to publish a book of sermons and attempt to give proper acknowledgement to those who have assisted in the production requires a "division of the house."

On one side of the house we acknowledge the specific shaping forces or personalities that form the fertile soil nourishing the preaching effort. Hyde Park Presbyterian Church, where these sermons were preached, is a congregation that listens with eyes, ears, and minds. They laugh, ask questions, seek more information, take suggestions, and sometimes disagree with the preacher. They are healthy participants in the preaching experience. During this series the Chancel Choir, under the leadership of Organist/Director Bonnie Gregory, was extremely supportive by singing Psalms set to familiar hymn tunes and leading the congregation in a wide variety of oral readings, all based on the Psalm of the day. They occasionally became a speech choir as we adapted Psalms for antiphonal reading using both choir and congregation. On one occasion we divided the congregation and choir into three solo readers and three group sections. The result was similar to a Greek drama. These profoundly positive experiences, which added so much to the worship and preaching, cannot be brought to the written page. I also want to recognize two individuals who used their musical gifts and Christian maturity to nurture my understanding of church music. First, Ruth Carr Williams directed the youth choir at my church during my teenage years. We sang every Sunday night. The impression was formative. John Sims, Director of the Male Chorale during my seminary training, taught me the value of quality professional leadership and the necessity of practice, even for those who are very good at what they do. As this sermon series progressed, I realized in a new way how much my preaching on Psalms had been shaped by this group of God's servants.

The other side of the house consists of the specific team involved in the production process. The idea of putting this series into book form began with the suggestion of Don Lawson, friend and nearby pastor, as we carpooled to a lunch meeting. Our conversation took place long before the actual preaching. I was just floating an idea by a fellow preacher. He asked some penetrating questions and then said, "You ought to do it—and put it in a book." Several months later, after I had abandoned the idea of printing the series, Hatty Lenfestey, one of the more astute listeners in the Hyde Park Church, gave me a mini-lecture on why she thought the book should be written. Afterwards, I felt guilty for wanting to leave the series in only the oral form. A few days later, another party unknown to Hatty, suggested I put the series into book form. This party also offered to finance the project with two stipulations. First, the donor was to remain anonymous and second, the grant would need to go to a benevolent organization. If it were not for Don, Hatty and the anonymous donor, I doubt the book would exist.

Three other people from the congregation of Hyde Park Church have made outstanding contributions to this production. Artist Amanda Louise Donoho used her gift and youthful enthusiasm to produce the 18 drawings inside the book. After hearing most of the sermons as they were preached, she had to read each one carefully and make a drawing that would capture some aspect of the Psalm upon which the sermon was based. Jamie Reinke has carefully edited the work. She is a true professional and has caught an embarrassing number of errors. She has made my writing immeasurably better. My wife, Gretchen, has assisted in ways too many to name. She has been especially helpful with proofreading and computer issues, of which I am gifted at creating. Together it has been a great team. Any error, omission, or confusion found on these pages is mine. Any benefit or blessing the reader may receive belongs to God.

PREFACE

Clergy with regular preaching responsibility determine their sermon texts and subjects in a variety of ways. Often the congregation is left to wonder why a particular sermon came to life at a specific time. I believe it will be helpful to the reader to understand the three streams of thought that merged almost simultaneously in my own mind and gave rise to this series.

A few months before these sermons were planned, I was impressed with an observation I read in a denominational periodical. The phrase, perhaps remembered inaccurately, made observation that Jesus did not mention the word "God" very often. He almost always used the term "Father." Not thinking much of it at the moment I lost track of its source. Nevertheless it hung around a long time in my head before homiletic juices began to flow. It caused me to ponder the various ways Jesus, in His humanity, learned about God.

The second stream of thought came from several long discussions I have had with my son, a classical pianist, performer, and teacher. It is only incidental that he is a church organist. These discussions focused on how music influences the development of the brain in young children. There is now much evidence that exposure at an early age to musical training leads to early brain development, resulting in a lifetime advantage over those who do not have this musical experience. Could there be a connection between the musical experiences of Jesus and his developmental understanding of God?

The third stream leading to this particular sermon series occurred when the Hyde Park Presbyterian Church and its pastor, Dr. Kenneth Shick, asked me to assume the pastoral responsibilities during Ken's four-month sabbatical. Preaching would move very close to the top of all my priorities, but nobody made any suggestions to me about subjects, emphasis, or issues to be addressed. The period of time was January through April, 2004, which would include Lent and Easter. I was already on the church staff as part-time Parish Associate. The church was in "good shape." Ken was to return from sabbatical to continue his 20-year ministry. The church did not need healing. It would not be my role to attempt innovative changes or start social crusades. I needed to keep the ship going in the direction it was headed, until the captain returned.

The three streams mentioned above merged in my mind. Preaching should be very pastoral during these days. Since our church did not have a strong history in adhering to a lectionary, I decided to look into the Psalms for my primary preaching texts. During Lent and on Easter Sunday I would use the Psalm reading suggested by the Revised Common Lectionary. This decision would push us into appropriate sermon material for these special seasons in the Christian faith; they are Chapters 8-14 of this book. The other sermons would be based on Psalms that I had found particularly helpful to me, either personally or in ministry with somebody else. I did not try to meet any other criteria in this selection. The sermon development took place under this question: What could young Jesus, as a boy in Nazareth, learn about God by singing—or hearing sung—this Psalm with His family and friends on Sabbath and Holy Days?

In answering the above question I assumed Jesus and I had two things in common: humanity and, at one time, youth. As detailed planning for the series progressed, I was surprised at how long ago—or how young I was—when the Psalms began to make their impression on me. The genesis of this series actually began when I was 12 and memorized the 23rd Psalm along with one other verse: "Your word is a lamp to my feet and a light to my path." (Psalm 119:105) These sermons are offered with a prayer that they will put light in the dim and dark places where the reader might travel.

INTRODUCTION

It is often said that the Old Testament Psalms were the Jewish hymnal. Though it may be a bit of a stretch to say the Psalms were also the hymnal of the early Christians, it can be said that they were used as one of their songbooks. From the earliest days of the Church until now the Psalms were a part of the Christian Liturgy for corporate worship as well as a part of the devotional literature used in private nurturing of faith. For the most part, priests, clergy, and choirs were the ones who did the singing during the first 15 centuries of church history. It was not until after the Reformation led by Luther, Calvin, and others that congregational singing gained common acceptance in churches. Even then it was accomplished with a struggle. Congregations generally used only the Psalter. Everybody would sing, but only words from the Psalms. Isaac Watts, in the early 1700's, was the first person to have his "human composition" widely accepted although there were several writers, including Martin Luther, who had limited success during the 200-300 years before Watts. We can conclude from this brief history that singing the Old Testament Psalms comprised the vast majority of all church singing until about 250-300 years ago.

Technically a Psalm is a poem. It consists of measures and lines creating rhythm as they are read. The poems make frequent use of parallelisms, metaphors, similes, and hyperbole. Each single Psalm generally consists of some kind of an introduction, its major development or issue, and a conclusion that on occasions is a repeat of the introduction. There are many good books that examine these poems in great detail. This is beyond our purpose since we are looking at only a very few selected Psalms through a rather narrow window. (See the Preface.)

Several Old Testament Psalms are not recorded in the Psalter. Those that are form a wonderful anthology of 150 poems related to almost every experience Israel had throughout history. Since they are related to every important event in the life of Israel, they give us instruction and counsel about praise, thanksgiving, lament, success, failure, enemies, friends, kings, kingdoms, personal life, communal existence, celebrations, and bereavement. They may be either individual or communal in nature. Occasionally they seem to confuse singular and plural so they may be either.

Perhaps the outstanding characteristic of the Psalms is that they function as Scripture – God's voice to us – and they also function as our voice to God – prayer and Liturgy.

In this still young twenty-first century the Psalms continue to exert their influence on our religious life for the same reason they were so vital to the early church. Since churches began congregational singing in the days of the Reformation, every generation has composed its own music to sing the old words in a new way. Tunes come and go, but the words remain. For almost three millennia the Psalms have nurtured individual and corporate faith. They have touched both the mind and heart of millions. There are students of scripture, however, who get overwhelmed in their effort to establish individual authorship and circumstance for each Psalm. The inability to know who, what, when, where, and why issues for many of the Psalms is extremely complex and unlikely to be totally resolved by scholars. These problems should not prevent the Psalms from being the inspired word of God to us as well as our word to God. This "two way street of communication" is one of the unique characteristics of the Psalms. We do not have to know the exact reason for the writing of each one to benefit from their example, instruction, or counsel.

An examination of our personal habits and the modern supermarket will give us a metaphor of understanding for these inspired poems. Most of our trips to the market consist of routine shopping for familiar comfort foods. Frequently, we will add items to our baskets recommended by others or accidentally discovered as we wander up and down the aisles. These new and unfamiliar items may become standard fare on future trips. Whether or not we purchase only the familiar or become more adventuresome, we always find something good to eat. When we finally leave the store, we know there will be more the next time we visit. We are nourished on every trip. And we know it will happen again. And again.

CHAPTER 1
PSALMS, HYMNS, AND SPIRITUAL
SONGS FOR THE CITY

Psalm 113 and Ephesians 5:18-19

Those whom we would recognize to be practitioners of the Fine Arts have far more influence on us than we imagine. This is why the first group of people to be suppressed by dictators is the artists—poets, painters, sculptors, novelists, and musicians. These people influence minds, especially young minds, in ways that reach far beyond a lifetime. For instance, during this Christmas season and the preceding Advent how many manger scenes did you find that had three wise men along with the shepherds? Biblical scholars have long known the wise men did not arrive along with the shepherds but came many months, perhaps even as much as two years later. Where did we get the idea there were three wise men? There were three gifts, but how many of you give a favored niece or grandchild more than one gift at Christmas? We are dealing with the artists' interpretation of a scene as they envisioned it, rather than depending on good scriptural analysis. Many people, especially children, have believed that is the way it was because that is the picture they saw somewhere—in a painting, in sculpture, or in song.

In his recent book, <u>God: A Brief History</u>, John Bowker traces the development of the concept of "god" as it has evolved throughout several centuries. He affirms the observations of many students of antiquity that almost every clearly identified culture has been credited with using song, hymn, and dance to express their particular understanding of divinity and its role in their lives. Many have come to agree that music is the most powerful and influential of all arts. It has the ability to use the full range of human emotion, psyche, and intellect like nothing else. There is a song—a musical expression—for every imaginable intellectual or emotional feeling: happiness, joy, grief, frustration, hatred, depression, aggression, sensuality, hostility, gratitude, apathy, etc. This should not be surprising since archeologists tell us every culture they have ever studied, no matter how ancient, has had its own musical expressions. Though there may be exceptions by particular individuals, there are no exceptions if we are speaking of broad cultures. All people like to sing in some kind of measured rhythm and tonal structure.

Is it any wonder that Paul, when speaking to the churches in Ephesus, suggested they should let the Holy Spirit rather than wine fill them, and then resort to "psalms and hymns and spiritual songs" (Ephesians 5:19) to express their overflowing enthusiasm and fresh commitment? Many people have looked at this scripture and sought to turn it into a description of three distinct kinds of music. This effort has been largely futile because the early church did not seek to make such distinction. Even the Jewish community continued to compose "psalms and hymns" after the present Psalter was completed. The early church continued this same practice of singing the Psalms passed down from Jewish liturgy and composing new hymns and spiritual songs to continue the centuries old practice of the people of God singing about their faith. Some of these new compositions found their way into the New Testament.

Since the beginning of the church the Psalms, as they are found in the Hebrew Bible, have been a major source of music and prayers used in both Christian worship and teaching. There are at least 287 quotations of the Old Testament in our New Testament and 116 of these are from the Psalter. Jesus was the source of some of these quotations, not the least of which was from the crucifixion cross.

With the spirit of Christmas still in the air—as this is written we are still in the liturgical season of Christmas—it is fitting to ponder the fact of Incarnation. Jesus, born in Bethlehem, was fully God and fully human, real humanity and real divinity, a paradox because each is equally 100% true. If we let Him be human, we have to let Him learn some things. By the age of twelve, He knew enough to confound the religious leaders of the day. Where did He learn this? How did He learn it? What did He learn? We have little to go on except we can assume He was a good Jewish boy of His age and time. As a good Jewish boy He learned the religious culture of His day from His elders—in the temple, synagogues, festival days, and home schooling. Then, as well as now, Judaism was primarily taught through repetition of ritual as opposed to the catechism method used by the later Christian community. Jesus sang the Psalms—over and over as He heard them. From these Psalms, the ones in our Bible, He learned basic concepts about God.

There is still much we do not know about how we learn—that is how the brain functions in the learning process—but there are some facts we should consider. Already we have mentioned that every culture archeologists have ever studied allowed music to play a large role in their cultural practices. Whether for entertainment, education, worship, communication, or meeting some other need, music in some form has always been present. Currently, there are scientists, musicians, and medical personnel studying the interaction of musical training and other forms of learning such as higher math. An official in the New York public school system recently related in Parade magazine their experience that elementary schools with a strong fine arts program, especially music, obtained higher ratings than those that eliminated such programs. An acquaintance of mine, Father Patrick Reardon, priest in the Antiochian Orthodox Church, says he has memorized the entire Psalter but that he can only sing it—and it needs to be sung in the tones he learned it. As unlikely as it might appear, I think this might be why Paul suggested we devote ourselves to singing "psalms and hymns and spiritual songs." He thought it was important that we know them. Repeated use of words in poetic form set to meter and tone impress their thoughts, verbiage, teaching, and emotions upon our brains, hearts, and psychological beings in a way little else does. If done with sufficient frequency they become so deeply embedded in our memory bank they can never be taken away. These are wonderful resources to have when faced with temptation and troubles as well as times of joyous celebration.

Jesus, as a growing boy in Nazareth, had to have learned some things in this same way. He went to the Temple. He was around the synagogue. He heard and prayed the same prayers we hear and pray when we turn to the Psalms. Like all the children of His day, this is one of the major ways He learned about God. It is also one of the major reasons Jesus talked very little about God. He talked much about His Father because of the special relationship He had with the Father. He did not have to talk much about God because He and His contemporaries shared the same understanding and background. They all had learned about God through the same rituals, festivals, and celebrations where the Psalms were frequently used as both song and prayer. This practice was followed by the early Christian church and has continued until this day. Some groups make greater use of the Psalms than others, but those who neglect them do so to their own detriment. They are also ignoring Paul's specific suggestion.

In many ways the Psalms represent the general population of the Old Testament period better than any other Old Testament writing. There is great diversity and little systematic organization. They are filled with great poetry, surprising harshness, loving tenderness, occasional desperation, and abiding faith. Many individuals have found their literary beauty to be unsurpassed.

More than anything else, the Psalms give us a picture of ancient Israel at worship; a picture revealing their conviction that God is present in their common life as a people. This picture must not be forgotten. God is near, God is present, even on the rare occasions when their words reveal some doubt. (Why would they say such words in worship if they thought He was absent and could not hear?)

This conviction of the presence of God in the life of Israel permeates all their emotions and circumstances. In community worship, public celebration, and home schooling they used the Psalms to remember the divine nature of the law given to them by a divine God. If this was faithfully perpetuated, their story would be implanted in both the national and individual psyche. Israel and the succeeding generations would know God as deliverer, protector, and disciplinarian. They would also experience this kind of God as one who loved them and was concerned about both their national and personal affairs.

Dr. Page Kelley frequently reminded his students that the Psalms were "the prayers of troubled Saints." They were—and still are—prayers in that they are addressed to God. They are words of troubled people who are dealing with many situations which they cannot handle on their own, or which they do not understand. They are saints in that those who are expressing themselves in this manner are the people of God.

The bulk of the population of Israel learned and communicated these general teachings of the Psalms in their worship. The musical expression would be a very good tool for a largely illiterate people to use. The ability to retain the teachings would be enhanced. This experience, using poetry, tone, and meter, would gloriously praise God and effectively teach the general population. The ritualistic, repetitive, and melodic expressions would insure the passing of both the law and the will of God from generation to generation.

In Psalm 113 we encounter an example of the general understandings already presented. The story is that of a troubled woman who, because of her childlessness, would occupy a rather low status in the ancient Middle East. The God of Israel would elevate her far beyond the customary social and legal possibilities in Babylon ruled by the Code of Hammurabi. God's sovereignty would be above that of all others. If God could accept her, surely Israel could. Her unfortunate childlessness had nothing to do with her acceptance by God.

For the Christian it is worth remembering that this is exactly how Luke started his Gospel story: two childless women, Elizabeth and Mary, persons society might have missed, but chosen, accepted, and elevated by God. It's Christmas. He is here. It's also worth remembering that Matthew's Gospel records the singing of a hymn as they departed from the Passover meal, setting the background for the Christian sacrament of the Lord's Supper. Keeping with the ancient tradition of Israel, they probably sang Psalm 113. And now we gather at the Lord's Table for the sacrament. He is here. We sing and celebrate.

As we obey the words of Paul and "sing psalms and hymns and spiritual songs" we learn about God. We remember what we have learned, pass it along to the next generation, and give witness to our city, as did Jesus. What could be a more worthy goal of our worship?

CHAPTER 2
MAKING CHOICES

Psalm 1 and Matthew 7:13-14

The hour was late and I was tired but wide-awake at the airport watching the crowd. I did not want to miss my daughter and her family as they arrived for a Christmas visit. While seated between the arriving shuttle and the elevators leading to the baggage claim area, I had opportunity to observe several hundred people in the little more than an hour I was there. I was surprised and amused at the wide variety of dress displayed on the rapidly moving passengers—both those departing and those arriving. After boredom had thoroughly set in, I mentioned to the elderly lady next to me that the dress of the traveling public was considerably different than when she and I made our first plane ride. With an obvious smile and affirmative nod she responded, "They live in houses without mirrors." She understood what I was implying. It is a common human trait that at times we do not want to look at ourselves.

Any of the disciplines involving psychological counseling struggle with getting their clients to look inward at aspects of their personality, background, prejudices, and values. For a variety of reasons this can be an uncomfortable experience. The lady at the airport shared my opinion that the appearance of many people we had observed could be improved if they would just look at themselves. (As an aside comment, I believe many of the individuals appeared as they did in order to get others to look at them. In many instances this motivation would be an even more compelling reason for them to look in the mirror.) With this kind of thought in mind Shakespeare put into the mouth of Hamlet these words addressed to his mother: "Come, come, and sit you down; you shall not budge. You go not till I set you up a glass where you may see the inmost part of you."

For hundreds of years the Psalms have served as mirrors reflecting reality whenever we, God's people, look into them. Sometimes we are comforted. At other times we are challenged. Surely it was this same way with the adolescent Jesus. With just a bit of imagination we can believe this very first Psalm, the favorite of many Christians today, was instrumental in teaching Him that He could never remove Himself from the presence of God and that there would always be choices set before Him.

Many Christian interpreters of scripture have observed the progression of the pilgrimage described in the opening words of the first Psalm: walk-stand-sit. The vision is so clear and progression so common. While leisurely walking along, one listens to the counsel of the wicked: not yet a participant in the wicked, just getting a little information. The next step is to stand in the way of the sinners: now one is close enough that he might be identified with the crowd. Finally, the journey is complete: he sits in their seminars to become a disciple. (v.1) Herein lies the result of the accumulation of a series of small but unwise choices. It would be so much better if the pilgrim would "delight in the law of the Lord…and meditate day and night." (v.2)

We do not have to stretch our imagination to believe these words helped Jesus form His thoughts found in Matthew 7:13-14. "Enter through the narrow gate; for the gate is wide and the road is easy that leads to destruction, and there are many who take it. For the gate is narrow and the road is hard that leads to life, and there are few who find it."

The Psalmist spelled out these two choices clearly and followed it with two metaphors, tree and chaff. One way produces long and profitable life with much fruit. It becomes a symbol of stability, refreshment, and refuge. The other way is useless chaff soon destroyed with no noticeable benefit. It temporarily drifts into useless nothingness.

For both the Psalmist and Jesus the primary consequence of these choices was longevity vs. destruction. The New Testament picture of the way to longevity is through Jesus who specifically declared, "I am the way, and the truth, and the life." (John 14:6) As we respond to this choice—follow Jesus or choose another way—we have decided, as did the Psalmist, to become like the tree rather than the chaff. This is the really big choice eliminating many lesser choices. Meditating on the "law of the Lord" (that is choosing to follow Jesus) will remove many of the options placed before us if we were sitting in the "seat of the scoffers" (choosing a way other than Jesus). At the same time, the way of Jesus does not free us from choices. Life has often been described as a pilgrimage. Those who find themselves on the "way of the righteous" (v.6) will discover this way also has many forks in the road where various decisions of huge consequence confront us daily. How will we know which ones to choose?

For more than a half century I have found help in the suggestions given to a group of senior high school and college students by Dr. T. B. Maston, a seminary professor. Though I can't remember all he said, his basic outline has remained with me and I believe it has saved me much grief. Dr. Maston suggested we test our decisions by three standards. First, is the test of prayer. Can we subject our conclusion, the decision we have made, to prayer in which we sincerely ask God to bless and assist us in carrying out the decision we have made? Perhaps we are still at the fork in the road where there are alternatives. Can we ask God to bless each one equally? A negative answer to this question will raise a barrier we should not cross. It cannot be the way of Jesus if we cannot ask God to bless it.

The second test Dr. Maston suggested is that of universality. Would it be a good thing for all of God's people to make the same decision we are about to make? Think about your conclusion and then apply that conclusion to your sister, your parents, your pastor, your granny, your fiancée, or your spouse. Go global for a moment: would it be best if every group or nation made the same decision and behaved in the same way? What would happen if everybody had this same standard?

A third test is that of secrecy. Will you be willing for your decision or action to be made public? Will you let everybody you know and love know what you have done or are about to do? Keep in mind the difference between privacy and secrecy. Dr. H. Leo Eddleman was president of the college I attended. At one of our frequent and required chapel services he once reminded the student body that bathrooms and bedrooms have doors to protect privacy, not secrecy. Everybody knows what occurs in each place, but privacy is valuable. Secrecy is another issue altogether. It has no place in matters of ethics, morality, and the way of Jesus.

Remember the lady who said, "they live in houses without mirrors." As uncomfortable as it might be, we must look at ourselves. We will, as Paul said in I Corinthians, "see in a mirror, dimly" (13:12) but to see dimly is better than to refuse to look. Consider the series of tests and the wide variety of decisions you have to make in your social, family, or work situations. You have already made the decision to follow the way of Jesus, the way of righteousness, and to be like the tree planted by streams of water. (v.6) There are still options along the path. Where will you put your hands? What will you fix your eye upon with desire, admiration, and commitment? What will occupy a great amount of your mental capacity? To what activities or behavior will you devote your bodily presence and support? Where will your money be spent or invested? What personal or public activity will benefit from your energy or talent?

The specific questions might fade into broader societal and personal issues of political choice, religious differences, and economic philosophies. The tests are still applicable: Can you pray for God's blessing to be on your conclusion? Would it be right or beneficial for society if everybody made the same choice and followed your example? Would your chosen course of action require secrecy at any level?

Answers to these questions are not easily discerned at the personal level and get even more difficult when applied to large masses of people, especially when crossing national and ethnic borders. Jesus' response to this entire problem seems to be clear. More people will choose the broad way—chaff and destruction—than the narrow way—living tree and life. (Matthew 7:13-14) Minority status for the ones who choose to follow Jesus has been established. Community standards are likely to be wrong.

Jesus learned as a youth, from the Psalmist, prophets, and other traditions of Israel, that there would be choices of a moral, ethical, or religious nature. It would be easy for us to hide behind His divinity and say there were few choices for Him. If He was fully God and fully man, as the ancient creeds pronounce, we can benefit from allowing His humanity to become obvious in this learning process. Surely the first Psalm would have been one of the chief pieces of curriculum for Jesus. He, like many of His peers, learned how important it was to "not follow the advice of the wicked, or take the path that sinners tread." (v.1) Rather, His "delight" should be "in the law of the Lord." (v.2) Constant attention to this law would help him stay in the "congregation of the righteous." (v.5) In this place, he would learn "the Lord watches over the way of the righteous, but the way of the wicked will perish." (vv.5-6)

Scholars of many disciplines have studied history, religious and secular, across the centuries. There may not be unanimous opinion, but there seems to be general agreement on one fact. When we think of time in terms of generations rather than years, and groups of people in broad geographical demographics rather than clans or nations, good seems to prevail. It is rather obvious that the Psalmist believed a "tree planted by streams of water" (v.3) would prevail over "chaff that the wind drives away." (v.4) As they say, "in the long run..."

Some of the real blessings God has given the church are apt teachers, spiritual leaders, gifted clergy, insightful prophets, passionate evangelists, and inspired Psalms, hymns, and spiritual songs. Together they help keep us in line with the good, "the way of the righteous." (v.6) It is not always an easy choice to make—but it is always the right choice to make.

CHAPTER 3

THE PLACE OF PEOPLE IN CREATION

Psalm 8 and Hebrews 2:5-9

During the early stages of preparing this sermon, I was in a conversation with a friend about environmental issues when he stated something I had never heard before from him. It revealed much of his concept about creation: ". . .the place of people in the world, equal to animals, or plants, or whatever." He was not sure of any kind of hierarchy in creation. I don't know if I had ever before talked with anybody who thought everything in creation had equal value. We did not pursue his line of thinking, but I certainly did not forget it. My guess is that he is not alone in this kind of thought.

Not long before the above conversation I had been reading about a baby born on Christmas Day, 1642. He was a small child and his father had been killed shortly before his birth. He seemed destined for a life of difficulty. So it was with him—a hard life filled with many misfortunes. In spite of this hard life, he was always filled with curiosity, such as wondering why the colors of the rainbow are always in the same order. After just a few years in school he demonstrated a superior intellect and motivation to excel in academic affairs. Along with this characteristic he always had a place for God, scripture, and teachings of the church in his thought.

Before he was a teenager he had read Descartes, Huygens, and Kepler. He made such enormous contribution to the scientific and philosophical thought of his era that today we recognize him as the primary moving force in establishing the entire field of study we call

"Natural Science." In spite of his great accomplishments, most of us remember him because of an apple that fell from a tree.

As the story goes, he, Isaac Newton, was lying on the ground late one evening watching the moonrise. He heard an apple fall from a nearby tree. He began to wonder. Why did it fall? Would it have fallen if the tree had been 100 feet tall? What about one mile? A hundred miles? Or from the moon? The boy thought about this for two decades before discovering the mathematical formula which allows us to explain, understand, and use this fundamental force in the universe we call gravity. Most of us will never really need the formula, $F = G \times M \times m \div d^2$, but I thought you ought to have it. This 350 year-old discovery of Newton's will help explain the spaghetti sauce that drops on your tie or NASA's ability to put the rover, Spirit, on Mars where it is rolling along at this moment.

Surely what is happening with such little things as spaghetti sauce on ties and such big things as rovers on Mars will help us understand there is a difference among humanity, plants, animals, and the God who has created all of it, even Mars and beyond.

As the Psalmist pondered the majesty of God (v.1), he saw God's place in creation to be so obvious that even "babes and infants" (v.2) could recognize it. We are hard pressed to look at nature and conclude the existence of God; but it is impossible to look at nature and conclude God is non-existent. Once we believe, as the Psalmist did, that God is present, all of nature reaffirms our belief. The work of people like Isaac Newton expands our horizons and the majesty of God. Slowly the door of understanding is opened, and we begin to see how humanity fits into the picture.

For Newton, the journey from a falling apple to the validated and accepted mathematical law of gravity took decades. From childhood curiosity to mature faith might also take decades. When it does, we know a clear difference between humanity and the rest of creation.

Science as an academic or applied discipline did not exist during the days of the Psalmist, but the ancient poets of Israel certainly understood, as we do today, that the Creator was not the created. The opening pages of the Psalter are devoted to individual prayers. Psalm 8 is the first one devoted only to praise and addressed solely to God. The words are a vigorous presentation of the separate and unequal natures of the creator God and the created humanity. Some people have looked at its words carelessly and concluded it is tainted by a pantheistic philosophy. A more careful analysis reveals the Psalmist is very firm in drawing the distinction between God and the rest of creation. It is also certain the Psalmist was speaking of all humanity rather than individuals. His subject is the relationship of "we" and "us," not "I" and "me," to God. The goal of the poet is to help us understand our smallness with severe limitations when compared to the God of creation.

The Psalmist said God made us "a little lower than God" (v.5) and that humanity has "dominion over the works of your (God's) hands," (v.6) including other animals, fish, birds, etc. Here we find a three-tier hierarchy of creation: God above, humanity a little lower, then the rest of God's handiwork. This is where we are in relationship to creation. We are not God, but subjects of God helping manage the rest of creation.

The partnership between God and humanity is best understood in light of the Incarnation of Jesus, who, according to the ancient church creeds, was made man. Being fully God, He was also fully man. It is easy to get confused at this point, because He was neither "a" man nor was He "all" men. If He had been "a" man, nothing would separate Him from any other man. If He had been "all men," He would have been another Noah doomed to repeat the same errors.

The writer of Hebrews said, "we do see Jesus, who for a little while was made lower than the angels, now crowned with glory and honor because of the suffering of death, so that by the grace of God he might taste death for everyone." (Hebrews 2:9) Jesus is then immediately identified as a "pioneer" (v.10) of salvation. These images fit nicely with John's Gospel which presents the idea that Jesus was the word made flesh and the agent of creation. (John 1:1-3) They also fit with the opening pages of Genesis where God's speech causes humanity, made in God's own image, to come into existence. (Genesis 1) The convergence of all these images help us understand that Jesus was the model God desired from the beginning. He was the first pattern for humanity. He was not an emergency vehicle later designed because humanity fell into sin. With this understanding of the Incarnation and of Psalm 8, we have to conclude the poet said more than first appears in a simple reading of the words. He was really writing about God, all humanity, and the entire work of Jesus, the Son of God.

Isaac Newton would probably be very surprised at how we have used his observations about gravity and advanced our scientific knowledge. But we have not advanced so far that some still wonder where humanity fits into everything else. From the earliest days of scripture through the Incarnation experience of Jesus until now, people of faith, based on the Judeo-Christian experience, have believed there is a hierarchy, with God the Father as supreme and with humanity a little lower but above all else in the created order. Cartoonists Jeff and Bil Keane pictured this in one of their recent drawings. A boy was sitting at a table eating his dinner. A nearby dog was salivating. The boy, refusing to share his food, observed that dogs don't eat people food because they are dogs. We live in a very complex ecosystem based on diversity and filled with thousands of creations placed here by God to sustain life. The biological terms of interdependence and symbiosis are scientific words that describe our need for the rest of creation. The fact that all creation is inter-related does not make each part of creation equal to any other part. Humanity, created in the image of God, is still the apex.

As a young man, Jesus learned that He and all other people were subject to the supreme creator, the God of Abraham, Isaac, and Jacob—the God who delivered the people from bondage in Egypt through the Exodus experience. He also learned about the equality of people as they worshiped and served the God of Israel. Further, He learned to respect but use the rest of the created order around Him.

These ideas may have come to Him from a variety of sources, but were routinely reinforced as the faith community worshiped and celebrated their festive occasions, singing and praying the Psalms.

This gave Him a foundation which would allow the more mature expansion and development expected from a youth who "increased in wisdom and in years, and in divine and human favor." (Luke 2:52)

From a very practical point of view, the 8th Psalm addresses one of the more prominent problems in modern society: low self-esteem, or perhaps an ego problem. We hear much about it, especially about children in an educational system where many say building self-esteem is the most important objective. Without debating the merits of their argument, examine what this Psalm teaches us. Humanity is just a little lower than God (v.5), but certainly is not God. (vv.1,5,9) There is no confusion here. Humanity is above the rest of creation. Again, no confusion.

If we take Hebrews 2 seriously, we will conclude even more about the nature of humanity. Jesus, the model of what God had in mind when we were created, left His heavenly home to come to earth and give us another chance to get it right. He lived among us, died for us, was raised again by the Father to provide a new way for us, and is now back where He came from—heaven—waiting for us to join Him there. He did this for all of us, just as He did it for each of us. That realization ought to help anybody's ego and self-esteem issues. This is a folksy metaphor, but the cargo has to be very valuable for God to go to that extent to make sure it gets to the right place.

Certainly humanity is more than an economic machine, as some political systems would have us believe. Humanity is more than a bundle of sexuality, as others might believe. We are certainly not a cosmic accident. Modern mathematical theory even identifies the odds as being too great for that to have happened. Can any serious thinker believe humanity is just an equal part of all other parts found in creation..."or whatever?"

Psalm 8, perhaps more than any other Psalm, helps us know our rightful place in creation. It may have been the beginning place for Jesus in the human development of His own self-understanding. It is a grand place for us to meditate—especially on the One "made man" for our own earthly benefit and eternal destiny.

CHAPTER 4

CERTAIN DILEMMAS IN LIFE

Psalm 107 and 2 Corinthians 4:7-10

It is a common experience for people of all cultures and religious experience to face certain dilemmas in life. I use the word "certain" to mean both experiences we hold in common *and* assurance that these will occur. A little history will help us understand what Psalm 107 teaches us about this commonality in life.

God promised Abraham that he, because of his faithful response to God, would become the founder of a new nation and that this nation would be established in a land not yet identified to Abraham. In this simple yet profound act of faith, Abraham began his journey to the Promised Land where his descendants would be many and the nation would flourish. As things later developed, Abraham's family journeyed to Egypt to escape a famine. He and his immediate family never left this land. In fact, they were there for about the next 400 years. God eventually used Moses to lead these descendants of Abraham out of Egypt in what we call the Exodus, a trip that took 40 years. During this period God gave the Ten Commandments to Moses. After finally reaching the Promised Land, the Kingdom of Israel was eventually established. When King Solomon died, about 921 BCE, the Kingdom split between the north, called Israel with Samaria as the capital, and the south, called Judah with Jerusalem as capital. In 722 BCE the Assyrian Empire—identified with present day Syria—conquered Samaria. This was followed in 586 BCE with the conquest of Jerusalem by Babylon— identified with present day Iraq. Babylon's foreign policy toward Israel led to the deportation of Israel's most capable and influential leaders. In fact, the major portion of Israel's population including the core leadership of all religious, political, economic, and educational personnel was transported to Babylon where they lived with a great deal of freedom but firmly under control of Babylonian rulers. Israel's worst nightmare had occurred: they had been removed from their Promised Land. They remained in this foreign land until King Cyrus, the Persian conqueror of Babylon, allowed them to return in 539 BCE. The period of time from 586-539 BCE is called the Babylonian Captivity.

Although Israel was displaced during the half century of captivity, it was a fruitful period of prophetic and poetic development. We believe Psalm 107 was composed almost immediately upon their restoration to the Promised Land in 539 BCE. It certainly expresses the concerns and dilemmas presented by the Babylonian Exile. During this time they wondered: What happened to God, the God who was supposed to be with them always? Why were they subject to such treatment since they were trying to follow the way God wanted them to go? Why was life so difficult for them?

The Psalmist addressed four large categories of problems his nation encountered during this time. Verses 4-5 describe those who "wandered in desert wastes...hungry and thirsty" and weak in spirit. This is what happened during both the exodus and exile. Verses 10-12 describe those who "sat in darkness and in gloom" of prison cells with "their hearts...bowed down with hard labor." These were common experiences during the exile period. Verse 17 portrays the sick, a normal occurrence in all societies, but an especially prominent problem during times of economic hardship and political instability.

Finally, in verse 23, the Psalmist describes those who "went down to the sea in ships, doing business on the mighty waters." The Israelites never looked very favorably upon maritime occupations. They were land nomads and city dwellers, not seamen. What they seem to be describing were occupations that were difficult, perhaps even undesirable. These words strike a familiar dilemma forced upon millions of laborers today—work that is difficult, undesirable, dangerous, and unhealthy.

Each of the problems the Psalmist described can be found on the front page of our daily papers or as lead stories on television network news.

Homelessness is a national problem and readily identified in any of our major cities. Hunger is an even greater problem, causing as much as one-third of our children in some states to go to bed each night hungry. Statistics are even worse in third-world countries. In light of all the political and economic discussions currently taking place about Medicare, Medicaid, health insurance, and drug costs can we find anybody who denies we have a problem related to our response to the those who are physically or mentally ill? The reference to maritime industry in the Psalm is really describing situations where people have to work in difficult, dangerous and unhealthy job categories they would not voluntarily choose. It is no stretch of the imagination to include current concepts such as downsizing, unemployable, minimum wage, child labor, and free-trade to social concerns this Psalm addresses.

The Psalmist personally knew these common experiences, made more demanding during the exile. With the passing of time, the nation was allowed to leave the exile and the difficulties of which the Psalmist sang became memories, but they were memories that must not be forgotten. The restoration of Israel called for celebration and attribution of their new blessing to their faithful God who was always present with them. For this, the Psalmist created a rejoicing chorus upon remembrance of these plaguing dilemmas: "Let them thank the Lord for his steadfast love, for his wonderful works to humankind." (vv.8,15,21,31)

The Apostle Paul provides us a more developed counsel on coping with similar situations in his correspondence with the Corinthian church. He was not in exile, but he had been put in jail because of his courageous preaching about the risen Christ. The church in Corinth was a very disturbed and dysfunctional congregation with several factions and moral issues. It even included people that seemed to rejoice by making mockery at Paul's prison experience. In the face of such persecution Paul needed to explain his abiding faith in Jesus and God the Father. He needed to explain how he could continue preaching the gospel in such circumstances. He attributed his ability to remain focused on his task to a "treasure in clay jars, so that it may be made clear that this extraordinary power belongs to God and does not come from us." (2 Corinthians 4:7) If he did not have God's help, he could not have dealt with the dilemmas and persecutions he suffered. He then proceeded to use four strong verbs describing dilemmas in his experience, and which also seem to occur frequently in our own. "We are *afflicted* in every way, but not crushed; *perplexed,* but not driven to despair; *persecuted,* but not forsaken; *struck* down, but not destroyed." (vv.8-9) Paul was able to survive these situations because he was "always carrying in the body the death of Jesus, so that the life of Jesus may also be visible in our bodies." (v.10)

God does not promise His people the deliverance from difficulties and uncertainties in life experiences. The circumstances of each situation may be different, but the emotional, physical, and psychological toll are common to humanity. God does promise His presence with us. God's revelation is that the best road to travel is the way of righteousness expressed in the Old Testament law, prophets, and Psalms, but more fully revealed in Jesus of Nazareth and made possible by His sacrifice. (v.10) Read again the four strong verbs mentioned above, and what Paul said happened in those situations: "not crushed... not driven to despair...not forsaken...not destroyed." (vv.8-9)

The ancient poet said more than he realized as he addressed the returning exiles over 2500 years ago. Jesus—and Paul—surely sang this Psalm as young lads learning about the faith of their fathers. They were never to forget their past. They were never to abandon God who was with them in every day and place of their lives.

Dr. John Claypool, one of my former pastors and one of the great preachers of this day, tells a wonderful story from the Chinese culture in one of his sermons. It is one of many stories which people have used across the centuries to help remember the commonality of life experiences. My memory of the details is fragile, but I am certain of the tale's core teachings. A farmer had only one horse. Used to till the soil and as a form of transportation, the horse was vital to the life and comfort on the family farm. One day as they were working the field something spooked the horse and it ran away. Trying as diligently as he could, thoroughly searching the hills and valleys, the farmer was unsuccessful in finding his run-away horse. Finally abandoning the search, the farmer returned to his home. He was soon greeted by friends and neighbors with universal concern and conviction that he had suffered a great loss and was destined to much hardship. Surprising those extending their sympathy, his response was, "good or bad—who knows?"

Several days later the farmer looked across the field and saw his horse approaching from the distance accompanied by a small herd of twelve more horses. Wild and untamed, they belonged to no one else. He could be rightful owner of a much larger herd brought to him by his run-away animal. Again the villagers surrounded him, but this time they brought glad congratulations and admiration at his good fortune. "You are most blessed. This is a wonderful addition to your farm." His response was, "good or bad—who knows?"

Not long after the expansion of the herd the farmer's son took it upon himself to train the still wild animals so they could be used on the family farm. For a while the training went smoothly, but ultimately the situation changed. One of the wild animals, showing great strength and resistance, threw the young rider from his back, and, as a result, the farmer's son received a severely broken leg, requiring many months to recover. Neighbors and friends again gathered at the farmer's home extending their sympathy and lamenting at the farmer's bad luck. It was most unfortunate and even a bit tragic that the son had been so severely injured when things seemed to be going so well for the farmer and his family. The old farmer responded, "good or bad—who knows?"

It was only a few days after the injury that news arrived in the village telling them of a major war breaking out in a nearby area. Shortly thereafter the news became even more disturbing. Every young man in the village would be conscripted by the government to fight in the war. Only the young man with the badly broken leg would be exempt from this draft into military forces. A short time later a messenger came to the village with the dreadful news—every one of the young men from the village had been killed in battle.

From this story, as well as Psalm 107, the writings of Paul, and the crucifixion of Jesus, we can learn we are not wise enough to judge every situation correctly as to its "badness" or "goodness." This is God's work. We can also learn from these same sources that God, in the long run, is working all things out for good.

CHAPTER 5

CREATION AND LAW

Psalm 19 and John 1:1-3, 14

Since the launching of the Hubble telescope, hardly a month goes by without some article in the newspaper telling us about a new discovery in outer space. New galaxies and previously unknown constellations are continuing to excite astronomers. We are even discovering new planets within our own solar system. NASA has a man-made robot roaming across the surface of Mars. It's a big universe out there—and our comprehension of how big it is expands every day.

The grandeur of the universe is also reflected in how small things are. The world of sub-atomic particles is constantly expanding. Things we were taught a half-century ago could not be divided into smaller parts have now been divided several times. We keep finding more and more as we explore the exciting world within the atom. It seems there is no way of reaching the edge, whether we look beyond our former boundaries or within the things we know.

On a daily basis we encounter life experiences causing us to wonder about creation and law. Issues related to space exploration, sub-atomic physics, stem-cell research, or world terrorism cause people from all strata of life to wonder about creation and law. How are they related? Are there universal laws and truths? What do we do if some of these seem to conflict with others? Why did God "do it this way?" Can we be sure there is a God? If ever there was a God, is He/She still around? Still involved?

With these questions wandering around in our minds we turn to Psalm 19 to discover how the ancient poet of Israel dealt with similar issues. The first part of the Psalm focuses on the natural world. Using few words, the Psalmist proclaimed as truth an observation we have heard believers across the centuries repeat. Just look at the heavens. Look at the starry sky on a cold clear winter night, examine the beauty of sunset over the ocean or mountain plains, wonder at the birth of a baby, or the intricate weaving of various tissue of the brain and you will have to believe in God. Theologians call it general revelation. Paul wrote about it, especially in his correspondence with Rome. Without a vocal sound, these wondrous testimonies from nature speak volumes.

The joyous repetitiveness of this testimony is illustrated by a common occurrence. A bridegroom comes out of his bridal chamber at sunrise with new joy and vigor. He goes about the day's activities as if life itself was beginning again. In the same way, the sun rises with a new brightness announcing a fresh day (vv.5-6) and God's glory is revealed once more. There is no place to hide from this testimony. (v.6) All who observe a simple sunrise see and hear what God has done, yet no words are spoken.

Even more important than this general or natural revelation is the law of God. For the ancient Israelites the law was much more than the Ten Commandments Moses received on Mount Sinai. We can best think of this law (*torah*, in Hebrew) as the whole instruction God gave Israel. This would include the commandments of Moses, rituals developed by the priests, and customs and habits of the community.

In Psalm 19:7-10 there is a series of expressions, each one with a slightly different meaning, but each one with its own place in explaining how the law God gave Israel worked to benefit the entire society. Verse 7 indicates the law "is perfect, reviving the soul." In this sense, as mentioned above, the law is the whole instruction Israel received from God. This is followed by the "decrees of the Lord," which refers to the personal regulations God has given regarding his will for his people. "The precepts of the Lord are right." (v.8) Here the poet is describing particular rules of duty the people of God have. If followed, the heart will rejoice. "The commandment of the Lord" (v.8b) is an imperative of the Lord which we most often equate with our concept of law. Obedience to this law is "enlightening" to our eyes. (v.8) The "fear of the Lord" (v.9) is a way of reminding us to remain in awe or respectful submission to God. It prevents us from assigning this place to anyone other than God. "Enduring forever" (v.9) reminds us this relationship will never change. Finally, the Psalmist tells us "the ordinances of the Lord are true." (v.9b) These are the regulations governing our relationships with our neighbors. These very relationships and rules are, according to the Psalmist, "righteous" (v.9) and "more to be desired…than gold, even much fine gold." (v.10)

Ancient Israel, believing that God had been personally involved in forming their nation and its customs, had no difficulty in linking laws, testimony, precepts, commandments, fear of God, and ordinances into the single basket of controls and regulations placed upon them by God. We do much the same today, but use a different set of words. We speak of laws, customs, folkways, habits, fear of God, and mores. Though each of these terms has its own specific meaning, we frequently encounter an area where they overlap in such a way that it is difficult to distinguish the beginning of one from the end of the other. Use your own mind at this point to build your own illustration. Think of almost any mode of dress, perhaps a thong bikini. Think also about a beach, church service, formal reception, county commissioners' board meeting, backyard party, and bedroom. This item of clothing can run the gamut from unlawful to customary, to acceptable, to habitual, and then desirable depending on…well, you get the message.

Taking Psalm 19 at face value reveals how God has disclosed Himself in natural (general) revelation (vv.1-6) for all to see and hear; but that revelation has not been as complete as revelation in the law. (vv.7-10) As good and beneficial as the law is for the people of God, it is also inadequate. The Psalmist speaks for all Israel as he acknowledges he, with the help of these wonderful gifts, cannot get right with God. Forgiveness is still needed. Another opportunity is necessary.

The poet was very correct in reminding us these laws exist as a warning. (v.11) He acknowledged society functions better when the group has a common basis of laws and customs to guide their relations with each other. "In keeping them there is a great reward." (v.11) We could easily get sidetracked at this point and discuss "good" laws vs. "bad" laws, various forms of political systems, or even civil vs. religious laws. Although law in ancient Israel was subject to an evolutionary process, the Psalmist did not enter into that debate. He was content to assume the community understood the basic concept. Law had come from God. It was for the benefit of the entire community. But it was inadequate.

"But who can detect their errors?" (v.12) The Psalmist was having trouble knowing whether or not he had sinned. This trouble confronted him at two points. First, the "hidden faults" (v.12) were errors made without understanding. Due to ignorance or lack of experience a mistake had been made. Thus he prayed, "Clear me from hidden faults." Second, there were the "insolent" (presumptuous) sins." (v.13) This indicates sins the Psalmist knew were wrong but out of arrogance, selfishness, or godlessness were still a part of his behavior. He knew better but did not act like it. (It is worth noting this behavior is not always limited to teenagers.) Thus the Psalmist prayed that God would not let these sins have "dominion" over him, thereby he could be "blameless, and innocent of great transgression." We can even say the Psalmist believed sins of presumptuousness were worse than sins of ignorance for they were of "great transgression." (v.13)

The Psalmist's prayer reaches its greatest maturity and theological depth as he utters to God, "Let the words of my mouth and the meditation of my heart be acceptable to you, O Lord, my rock and my redeemer." (v.14) Here it is clearly acknowledged that the general (natural) revelation and the law are both insufficient to cleanse away the sin of error or presumption. As beneficial as general revelation and natural law are to the community of faith, only God can redeem.

Perhaps the most interesting thing about this Psalm is that the poet's focus is on his words and meditation. Not unlike songwriters of today the Psalmist knows the work of his heart and mind unite in forming the words which are spoken. Words from the mouth come from the heart. They are nurtured by meditation prior to expression. The challenge is to always make them "acceptable" (v.14) to God.

Some of the earliest commentaries on this Psalm indicate it may have served as the foundation for Psalm 119, the longest in scripture. Many early Jewish scholars and some of the early church fathers considered the entire Old Testament to be God's law for Israel. Building on this concept and using Psalm 19 as a guide, another poet penned Psalm 119 in a rather unusual manner. He took each letter of the Hebrew alphabet, in its normal sequence, and constructed a verse using that letter to begin the first line of each stanza. Since the Hebrew alphabet has 22 letters there are 22 stanzas, beginning with *aleph*, the first letter, and proceeding through *wah*, the last letter. The result is highly symbolic. Using the entire alphabet in sequence implies that every word in the language may and should be acceptable to God. Certainly all scripture is holy, righteous, and acceptable to God. The words from our own lips ought to follow this example, which is exactly the prayer of the Psalmist. (v.14)

As Israel used these two Psalms, 19 and 119, in its liturgy and holy celebrations, Jesus would have been exposed to this understanding of law and the accompanying teachings of His people. The unspoken words of general revelation found in nature as well as the many spoken words of law would all be acceptable to God, a warning to his people, and beneficial to society. But there must be more, because the prayer of the Psalmist was that God would do something to correct the sins of error (ignorance) and insolence (presumptuousness and willful disobedience).

As we have previously observed, Christians must not read the Old Testament as if the New Testament was non-existent. The prayer of the Psalmist was answered with the birth, life, death, and resurrection of Jesus. On the very first page of the Old Testament the writer declares God's creation began when God spoke. "And God said." (Genesis 1:3,6,9,11,14,20,24,26,28) Answering the prayer of Israel's best poet, the Creator who did His work by speech came to earth, in human form, described in John's Gospel as the "Word became flesh." (1:14) The New Testament and its entire story is God's answer to the Psalmist's prayer. And ours also.

CHAPTER 6

FORGIVENESS (RENEWAL)

Psalm 51 And Romans 8:1-8

Many students of scripture believe David, King of Israel and ancestor of Jesus, is the most outstanding figure in the Old Testament. Noted poet and warrior, he united the Kingdom of Israel and expanded it to its greatest grandeur. He is also recognized as an outstanding example of fleshly sin, repentance, forgiveness, and renewal of life. Reflecting upon his life experiences may lead us to conclude he is the king of second chances. Tradition attributes Psalm 51 to him and is said to follow his discussion with Nathan about the Bathsheba affair. Though there is some doubt concerning David's authorship, there is no doubt that this Psalm accurately describes the experience of David, Bathsheba, Nathan, and God.

The scriptures (2 Samuel 11) tell us that David just happened to look out his palace window and saw his neighbor, Bathsheba, bathing in a rather revealing manner. Even though she was at home, she was exposed and King David liked what he saw. Knowing her husband, Uriah, was away at battle, he invited her to his palace. The seventh commandment was broken, she returned to her home, and not too long after that fateful afternoon she sent word to the King that she was pregnant. David immediately ordered Uriah to report to the King's palace. Upon his arrival David suggested that Uriah go to his home, spend time with Bathsheba, and enjoy a brief holiday. Uriah did not do as David instructed. Instead, he chose to remain with his fellow soldiers because they were not offered equal leave. David was upset at Uriah's decision. He again invited Uriah to the palace. An elaborate feast was made, during which Uriah became drunk. Even in the state of drunkenness Uriah chose a second time to remain with his soldiers. David was angry and vindictive. He ordered Uriah's return to Joab and battle. As commander, Joab was instructed by David to assign Uriah the most hazadrous duty. Further, Joab was specifically told to make sure Uriah could not return home. Joab did as the King ordered, and Uriah, along with several other servants of David, was killed in a useless battle. Following the appropriate period of mourning, Bathsheba moved into the palace with David as one of his wives. Not long after this event unfolded, God sent his prophet, Nathan, to confront David with his behavior. David confessed, repented, and God forgave. But, from time to time David had many problems with a dysfunctional family largely due to the series of events related to Bathsheba. In this one episode David was successful in breaking at least half of the Ten Commandments of Moses: covetousness, adultery, theft, murder, false witnessing. What a sorry tale!

There is probably no place in the Psalter, or maybe even the Old Testament, where we can get better insight into the nature of sin than Psalm 51. Though the Psalm begins as the experience of one individual, we must hear it as a description of humanity. In the first few lines of the poetic prayer the Psalm presents four distinct words to describe the sin of David—and humanity. *Hata* (v.2) is the basic word for "sin," meaning missing the target or getting lost. It is being habitually against God or the nation and can refer to religious or civil action. Also in verse 2 we find *awon,* translated "iniquity" and understood to mean personal guilt or culpability. The word "transgression" in verse 3 translates *pesa* and describes a willful rebellion of national or moral behavior. *Ra* in verse 4 is translated "evil," meaning moral or unethical behavior injurious to others. It is the opposite of good.

Whoever prays this prayer, whether David a thousand years before the birth of Jesus or first time readers of the Psalm today, must consider the words in verse 4, "Against you, and you alone, have I sinned," to be the key insight brought to us by this holy writer. The words reach a height of spiritual maturity seldom attained. Sin is against God before it is against others. Sin is a failure to honor God before it is a disrespect of self or others. It is good to remember our standard for righteousness is not a standard we construct but a standard God presents to us. It is a standard coming from divine revelation, not a neighborhood code developed by our friends. It derives from a God who is always present and who clearly has repeatedly warned us against straying from God's way.

We can easily understand the criminal who carefully plans the murder or bank robbery before pulling the trigger or tunneling through the bank walls. We know how somebody might devote much time and thought to develop a financial scam based on illegal maneuvering of checks and cash through various businesses and banking institutions. We may find it more difficult to imagine somebody dwelling on fantasy relationships with the opposite sex or even simple investigations into ways they can unlawfully avoid tax payments. But when we carefully consider human behavior, we conclude very little is done without thought. Even most of our reptilian behavior, generally said to be impulsive, is developed based upon our previous experiences and what we have thought about them. Though we have no Biblical evidence to prove the point, we might even suspect David knew exactly where and at what time to look out the window for Bathsheba. She might even have planned to put herself on display. Again, we don't know this to be Biblically or historically true, but it is the kind of behavior sin creates.

Long ago, there was a popular song, "Little Things Mean A Lot." So it is with sin. Even the little sins are against God before they are against our human relationships, because they start in the heart and mind. They cause us to become less than God wants us to be. Then we act, bringing even more harm to others and ourselves.

The story of how this insight was revealed to David is found in 2 Samuel 12:1-6. It is a classic all of us should recall from time to time for our own benefit. God sent his prophet, Nathan, to tell King David of two men, one rich and one poor. The rich man had many animals on his vast farm whereas the poor man had only one female lamb. The poor man's lamb was dear to him, and he loved it devotedly. One day a traveler came to the home of the rich man. As mealtime approached, the rich man, refusing to sacrifice one of his animals for the required hospitality, took the poor man's lamb and turned it into dinner. Upon hearing this tale David became angry at the rich man and declared to Nathan, "As the Lord lives, the man who has done this deserves to die." (v.5) Nathan's response to David is one of the classic examples of prophetic utterance: "David, 'you are the man!'" (v.7)

In conversation following this declaration, David uttered the basic prayer of confession used by God's people for three thousand years: "I have sinned against the Lord." (v.13)   David's confession was probably used by the Psalmist to write the opening words of Psalm 51, "Have mercy on me, O God, according to your steadfast love; according to your abundant mercy blot out my transgressions." (v.1) This admission of sin, and the dependence of the sinner upon the grace and mercy of God, became the essential concept forming the basis of Psalm 51. These words, said by some to be the most frequently used scripture in corporate worship, work their way into our formal prayers of written liturgy as well as our informal expressions: "Have mercy on me, O God,...and cleanse me from my sin." (vv.1-2)

The Psalmist, having become aware of personal sin, then became aware of God's presence and the need for divine forgiveness. A series of verbs are used by the writer in verses 7-12 to describe what the Psalmist wants God to do for him as a result of his sin. Each verb is followed by a result the Psalmist expects: purge, wash, fill, hide, create, cast, and restore. The Psalmist needs to be re-created. The forgiveness of God can bring a remaking, a complete renewal of the one praying this prayer. Here we stand at the peak of the Old Testament understanding of human sin, God's forgiveness, and its positive result.

Although the Psalm seems to have been born out of an individual experience, there are several components leading to a clear understanding of its communal nature. The Psalmist has used all the words commonly used in Hebrew to identify an offense against God: sin, transgression, and iniquity. Many of the expressions fit the time and vocabulary used by Jeremiah, Ezekiel, and Isaiah, personalities who lived long after David. The last portions of the Psalm refer to teaching transgressors (v.13), singing about the deliverance (v.14), making burnt offerings (v.16), going to make sacrifice (vv.16-17), rebuilding the walls of Jerusalem (v.18), and right sacrifices. (v.18) As a whole, these expressions lend themselves to this Psalm being a fitting prayer for the entire faith community. It describes the experience of the group as well as the individual, and it is appropriate to use in the liturgy of the community as well as on prayerful knees beside one's bed. The strange words of verse 5 related to conception and birth, "I was born guilty," are not a description of our sexuality, but a description of our human experience wherein we all sin. The prayer describes sinfulness, not just a few sins. It acknowledges our need of God's mercy, not just our offerings of cash or good works. The seriousness of this need is reinforced by the use of a Hebrew word in verse 14, translated bloodshed. It is a sin that caused death and will lead to the death of the sinner.

The prayer of the Psalmist is that God will show mercy upon him by changing *him* rather than his environment. His problem is sin, not sins. It is of his making and not the fault of others. This requires the creative power (v.10) of God. Just as God created all things out of nothing, even so the Psalmist needs this same creative experience— God bringing something into his life that has not existed before. In the closing portions of the Psalm the poet recognized sacrifices and burnt offerings are not enough. This recognition is applicable to the community of faith as well as the individual. It is a "broken and contrite heart" (v.17) God requires. This phrase is the writer's way of saying his body, his will, his mind, and his psyche are all presented to God. Nothing is being held back. Again, this is applicable to both the individual and the faith community. It is how the "walls of Jerusalem" (v.18) will be restored and how its individual citizens will be cleansed. (v.2) It was a good thing for Jesus to hear these lessons as a young boy.

Verse 11 is one of only two places in the Old Testament using the phrase "holy spirit." God's presence continued to be with the Psalmist, David, and the community of Israel. The new thing God had for the future was the coming of the Messiah, Jesus of Nazareth. This was the subject of Paul in Romans 8. "There is now no condemnation for those who are in Christ Jesus…God has done what the law…could not do." (vv.1-3) We, like David, confess our sin, known and unknown. Then a totally new life through Jesus Christ begins to unfold. That is real renewal—the work of the Holy Spirit. And we, like David, get a new start. It's just like being born again.

CHAPTER 7

HARD TIMES

Psalm 90 and Romans 8:22-23, 38-39

This Psalm is familiar to most people because of its frequent use in funeral or memorial services. The ancient church also used it as a daily reading. In the Eastern tradition it was used in the beginning of the day, while in the West it was used at the beginning of work. These common uses are related by one familiar constant: time.

Physicists, philosophers, and the general public all have a difficult task ahead of them when they attempt to write a definition of "time." It will be enough for most of us to just agree we know what we are talking about when we use the term. We have been culturally conditioned to think like the Greeks by dividing the concept into two parts. The first definition is related to the hands on the clock. It is a chronologically progressive division into hours, days, and years. The second part of the definition is to describe a state of affairs. The time is right to plant the crop, or the time is right for him to leave home and establish his own household. We understand these simple divisions. The writer of Psalm 90 was concerned about this latter use of time.

When I was born, the country and world were still recovering from the Great Depression, an experience my young friends probably have not even read about. The economic conditions were so severe and lasted so long that the most common phrase I remember hearing was "the times were hard." It didn't take an economist to know what these people were talking about. More recently the phrase has been used to describe the 60's and early 70's when there was so much civil unrest related to human rights issues and the Vietnam War. Occasionally, somebody would refer to that period of history as "hard times."

"Hard times" are not just experiences of the larger community. They can be individual in nature. They can also be of any duration— a day, a month, or a year. In our experience they can consist of illness, natural disaster, war, economic failure, mental instability, human betrayal, accidents, or moral lapses leading to poor ethical choices. Sometimes hindsight reveals we could have done something to prevent or lessen the impact of the causative factors leading to "hard times." On other occasions there seems to be no reasonable explanation of a way we could have avoided the "hard times" that are thrust upon us. In spite of all these causes, the Psalmist would have believed the basic reason for all "hard times" was sin—sin of the individual or sin of the community.

This would be a particularly perplexing problem for Israel because they believed "time" was linear rather than circular. The circular concept of time can be described as living on a wheel which will eventually return to the same point again. History will then repeat itself. It is commonly expressed by the passing of seasons. Whatever season you are in will eventually return. Israel rejected this view of time for the linear concept. History was going somewhere. There was a goal. There would be a climax. And God would be with them on this journey. The children of Abraham would reign over the nations, but this reign would be under God; and God would always be present. With this kind of belief system, how could they explain "hard times?" How could they endure "hard times?" Psalm 90, particularly vv.3-12, is a prayerful lament to God for help. This prayer is probably a private or personal expression that was extended to include the whole community. Some would even argue it was extended to be a prayer for the entire human race. The unselfish attitude provides all humanity an example of spiritual maturity. Prayers of the people should include all people.

The first portion of the Psalm, vv.1-6, reveals a key reality the Psalmist understood: we are mortal and God is not. "Before the mountains were brought forth, or ever you had formed the earth and the world, from everlasting to everlasting you are God....For a thousand years in your sight are like yesterday when it is past, or like a watch in the night." (vv.2,4) God is above and beyond time. (Genesis 1:3) This is why the Psalmist can pray to God, who is *his* creator as well as the creator of time.

The focus of Psalm 90:7-12 is God's wrath (anger) with our sin. How can he go on? How can he cope? How can he deal with the hard times he faces, not the least of which is his feeling that God is unhappy with him? He describes himself as being "consumed" (v.7) by God's anger. Somehow God has discovered the known sins as well as the "unknown" sins. (v.8) Now he feels destined to end his life with a "sigh." (v.9) There is nothing else he can do even if he were to live for an unusual length of time. (v.10) Here the Psalmist recognized God had been active in exposing his sin rather than excusing it.

Now, with sin exposed, the Psalmist, in verse 11, expresses great anxiety. As a result, he offers a new petition in his prayer, a petition we might call the most important insight found in this Psalm. God is asked to "teach us to count our days that we may gain a wise heart." (v.12). This prayer is both personal and an example of how the personal lament has been applied to the entire community.

When we ask God to teach us something, we should be willing to consider what God has already taught us. The writer of Psalm 90 could have been assisted by recalling the "two ways" before us. Just as a straight line is the shortest distance between two points, so is the straight and narrow the best path to our destination in the time God has given us. The God who is always with us (Chapter 1, this series) always wants us to follow this straight and narrow which leads to life, rather than the broad and crooked which leads to destruction (chapter 2, this series). One of the things I have learned by living a long time is that I make bad decisions—decisions that have consequences resulting in "hard times." I also recognize other people have the same problem. The following quotes come from real people—people that I have counseled. From a woman in her 40's struggling with her third marriage: "I have nobody to blame but myself. I have made three bad choices. And down deep in my heart

I knew each one was wrong." A high school senior, referring to his girlfriend: "I know I should not have hit her." A young professional, eager for business success, ignored family responsibilities, worked unbelievable hours, and watched his wife, with three pre-school children at home, deteriorate into a physical and emotional zombie: "I knew better but just had the wrong priorities." The treasurer of a benevolent youth organization embezzled funds: "I know it was wrong but I needed the money. I didn't think I would get caught before I could return it."

We can identify these sins easily. Most of us know they are likely to bring hard times upon us. More difficult to understand are social, economic, political, natural, and historical forces beyond our control. They too create hard times. But more often, it seems to me, hard times come due to conscious decisions we make. We overrule the inner voice warning us of the forthcoming disaster. We yield to a temptation we know we should resist. We act out of character and do what we know we should not. We shut our eyes and plunge full speed ahead on the broad and crooked way we have paved, knowing it is not the godly straight and narrow. Then we wonder why God seems far away and hard times are close upon us.

As the scriptures and creeds also express, there are sins we commit without awareness. Sometimes we just do not know what we have done. Our lack of knowledge about the natural world, social relationships, or even political judgments causes harm to come to both others and us. More likely, we set ourselves in the place of God, act as our own supreme ruler, become our personal source of ultimate authority, and sin abundantly. Unhealthy doses of selfishness and pride creep into our decision-making matrix. In these early years of century 21 this is a rampant pattern of behavior. The Bible, long before the days of Jesus, described such an era as everybody "doing what was right in their own eyes." (Judges 21:29)

The Psalmist struggled with issues of the type mentioned. He also struggled with issues of war, capture by a foreign nation, illness, natural disasters, and situations he could never understand. He was not unlike today's citizens in a world of poverty, violations of human rights, international conflict, terrorism, earthquakes, famine, and death. The longer he experienced these situations, the more useless his effort seemed. He appeared ready to give up. He drifted into an attitude of resignation. It was as if he could do nothing in the time allotted to him.

We do not know how old the Psalmist was, where he was in his time, when these words were written. Perhaps they are the work of one lonely poet. More likely they were shaped over a period of years and had the benefit of editorial consultants helping to form the final product we now possess. Maybe he had a few friends assisting him in his final choice of words as they pondered these things by open campfire under cold starlight. Our experience teaches us that the ancient—and present—concept of time being linear tends to push us through various stages. During youth it is easy to feel immortal or outside of time. "It can't happen to me." "I'm too strong; too young." "Party 'til you drop." "Speed limits are for the old folks—get off the road." "Hard times—they're for somebody else." During mid-life we work with a passion; give attention to the world's problems; concentrate on doing what is right; prepare for the future; educate the children; and look forward to retirement. But hard times still are with us. Then in our latter years we too often join the Psalmist with a "sigh," (v.9) creep into despair, and wait for our time to "fly away." (v.10) In the end, not much has changed.

We would be grossly unfair to the author of these insightful words if we did not notice the change of spirit in verses 11-12. In his search for survival techniques during hard times a final realization came. The source of his only help would be a merciful God. Clearly these final words are personal in that they are his experiences. But they also reflect the life experiences of the larger community. Time is still a great concern. "Satisfy us in the morning with your steadfast love, so that we may rejoice and be glad all our days." (v.14) As the Psalmist seeks to avoid hard times, he prays for an equal exchange of happy days. (v.15) There is no expectation of life beyond the grave. He will be satisfied with just a fair balance of good and bad days. To his credit, his prayer is for the whole community. There is no selfishness here. He wants all the servants of God and their succeeding children to benefit from God's mercy and relief from hard times. His final touch is a prayer for the accomplishments—work—of the people of God, including himself: "O prosper the work of our hands!" (v.17)

We might err in saying the Psalmist felt his work would put him in right relationship with God, his neighbors, and time. We would not err in recognizing his prayer was offered with hope but no assurance.

As always, reading the Old Testament leaves us with a partial message needing to be completed by the words of Jesus, His disciples, and the New Testament. In the gospels we find the full story of Jesus, the Son of God, fully human and fully divine. He is the one who has come to give us real and abundant life. (John 10:10) It is He who is the light of the world. (John 1ff) Even He experienced hard times. Before He reached His teenage years, we know He had to be relocated three times to avoid death. (Matthew 2) Early in His ministry He was run out of town, probably on more than one occasion. His closest disciples abandoned Him in a time of great need. One whom He had personally chosen to be a disciple placed the kiss of death upon His cheek. All agree He was unjustly executed in a most cruel manner. During this experience He even thought God had abandoned Him. He suffered for no earthly reason. Then God raised Him out of the grave. He came to life again. The resurrection was real. This is a hope the Psalmist never knew.

The writer of Hebrews, especially in Chapter 2, helps us understand the hard times and suffering of Jesus. By suffering, He was able to become the high priest making the one time offering necessary for our redemption. He removed the stumbling blocks between God and us. He perfectly executed God's plan to give us ultimate victory over the sufferings and hard times of life itself, even the experience of death. He became the pioneer (Hebrews 2:10) providing us the way to follow Him safely through time to the heavenly home from which He came. Jesus, Son of God, resurrected Lord, pioneer showing us how to live and how to serve God the Father, becomes the light we must follow. He is the answer to the Psalmist's prayer.

The work we do during the time God has given us will accomplish nothing if we do not have our eyes focused on the right goal. To follow and serve Him is that goal. We can be sure hard times will still come. We have no reason to expect we will be spared what every human being, even Jesus, has experienced. The ancient sea captain, explaining to the young sailor how he would navigate the harbor with its narrow channel and rocky shores on either side, said: "Look at yonder light on the hill. Now see the distant light from whence we came. As long as I stay on a straight line between the two I will arrive safely home."

As long as we focus on the resurrected Jesus, the light of the world, we will arrive safely home. The resurrection proved His immortality. That He suffered for us enables us to participate in the new life He offers. The resurrection delivers us to the Creator God, Father of Jesus and all humankind, to an existence above and beyond time.

It is this assurance the Psalmist did not have, but which has come to us by Jesus. This is why Paul could say, "No, in all these things we are more than conquerors through him who loved us. For I am convinced that neither death, nor life, nor angels, nor rulers, nor things present, nor things to come, nor powers, nor height, nor depth, nor anything else in all creation, will be able to separate us from the love of God in Christ Jesus our Lord." (Romans 8:37-39)

CHAPTER 8

THE BENEFITS OF WORSHIP

Psalm 91:1-6, 14-16 and Luke 4:1-13

When Senator Joe Lieberman ran for Vice President a few years back, most Protestant and "no religious preference" Americans were introduced to a new way of observing Sabbath. His Jewish Orthodox faith was the source of baffling behavior for most people in our culture, especially candidates for high political office. On Sabbath he walked to worship. He didn't work. He didn't make speeches. He didn't go to the office. He didn't even attempt to raise money. To him and his faith community, Sabbath was—and is—a day unlike other days of the week.

When Jesus sang the Psalms, He was singing in a culture that primarily taught their faith by the ritual observances they practiced. This included religious and civil celebrations of seasonal or annual occasion, as well as the weekly practice of Sabbath. In our present Western Protestant tradition we place most of our teaching in a methodology we call catechism. This difference of emphasis on how our traditions and core values are taught is one of the reasons Senator Lieberman's Sabbath observance was so important to him and so confusing to many other Americans.

Jewish converts to Christianity often experience this conflict. We might expect Sabbath observance to be readily exchanged for Sunday worship. For the serious practitioner of Sabbath this is not easily done. In the day of Jesus—and in Senator Lieberman's faith—Sabbath set the tone for the rest of the week. From the ritualistic practices of Sabbath the values, direction, and limitations of the following days would be derived. Life-style and work-style would be set by what was done or not done on Sabbath. It was a ritualistic educational experience rather than an intellectual pursuit. We cannot say Psalm 91 was written to tell us about Sabbath observance. We can note, however, the ancient church used this Psalm as a standard part of funeral services and as a daily reading.

Used in this manner we discover what may be the greatest confidence builder in the Psalter. The Psalm easily divides itself into two sections. Verses 1-13 are spoken by a person to those who "live in the shelter of the Most High, who abide in the shadow of the Almighty." (v.1) In verses 14-16 we read the words of the Most High, the Almighty, in whose shelter one is abiding. This Psalm uses a vocabulary common in the Psalter to describe what the Lord (Most High, Almighty) will provide: shelter, refuge, fortress, and dwelling place. These expressions explain benefits provided by God to those who are willing to trust Him. There is also in the Psalm a long list of dangers from which God will spare those who exercise this trust: snare of the flower, deadly pestilence, fear of the terror of night, arrows, destruction, punishment of the wicked, scourge, stubbing of the toe, lions, and adders. Many of these are hyperbole, while others may refer to magical concerns related to nearby cultures. Some may refer to supernatural powers. Taken as a whole, the Psalter declares that trust in God is the only way one can avoid becoming prey to a wide variety of disasters and anxieties. God is the only one who can provide permanent and constant protection.

These reassurances pass on to the Christian believer with the added blessing of hope found in the resurrection of Jesus. The typical Christian of today may not follow all the rules related to the ancient Sabbath. There are even wide differences in the practice of our Sunday observance, which is the best equivalence we have to Sabbath. But there is no doubt the Christian community believes the kind of trust and worship practiced by the Psalmist will have similar consequences in our own worship, whether it be private or corporate.

Jesus understood this. Worship and service to God would be based on trust of God rather than testing of God. One of the major maintenance devices of this trust would be repetitive and regular worship, which would include the singing and praying of these words. They would be embedded in His memory bank. They would serve Him well when Satan would seek to use them against Him.

One of the premises I have laid out in this series of sermons on the Psalms is that Jesus learned much of His understanding about God in the literature, worship, festivals, and the holiday celebrations of His religious faith. Jesus did not have full maturity at the beginning of His life. Luke said, "Jesus increased in wisdom and in years, and in divine and human favor." (Luke 2:52) As a normal boy, His growth process stretched over several years. These words, spoken when He was 12, are the last Biblical reference about Him until age 30, when He, according to Jewish custom, could begin a public ministry.

In a behavior strange to us, the first thing He did as a public ministry was to withdraw Himself for a period of 40 days into what the Bible termed a "wilderness," (Luke 4:1) perhaps best described as a desert. It was certainly a place of isolation, remoteness, and without any of the amenities of a comfortable life. There He fasted for a long period of time – forty days – trying to determine how He would accomplish the will of the Father who had sent Him into this world. In the middle of that struggle, Satan appeared and attempted to use the promises of Psalm 91 to shape the future ministry of Jesus.

Let me paraphrase the familiar story (Luke 4:1-13) a bit. Satan said, "Now you're hungry, aren't you? You've been here a long time – haven't had a value meal. No 'Big Mac,' nothing. Why don't you take one of these rocks and turn it into bread? You can surely do that." Jesus said, "It is written, 'One does not live by bread alone.'" (Deuteronomy 8:3) In a more contemporary expression: "I'm not going to do it that way. That's not the way the Father wants it. Don't tempt me."

Not being satisfied with this response, Satan took Jesus up into a high place. We don't know exactly where the place was, but the view was sufficient for Satan to expose all of the nations of the world to Jesus. When Jesus could get a good view of the geographical, economic, and political possibilities, Satan made the offer. "Now all of this has been given to me," Satan said, "and I can give it unto you. You can have the adulation, you can have the wealth, you can have the popularity, you can have the influence, you can have all of this for yourself. The only thing you have to do is worship me." The response of Jesus, "Worship the Lord your God and serve only him," (Luke 4:8) is a quote from Deuteronomy 6:13. Jesus again had told Satan, "I'm not going to do it that way."

Having heard Jesus quote from the scriptures, Satan decided to try the same tactic in a third temptation. He even went so far as to take Jesus to the pinnacle of the temple, a holy place in prominent view of the crowds. Drawing from Psalm 91, Satan said to Jesus, "If you are the Son of God, throw yourself down from here; for it is written, 'He will command his angels concerning you, to protect you,' and 'On their hands they will bear you up, so that you will not dash your foot against a stone.'" To this third temptation Jesus responded with another Biblical quotation: "Do not put the Lord your God to the test." (Deuteronomy 6:16) The conversation between Jesus and Satan ends about like it began: "No, I don't work that way. That is not what God wants." Then we see Satan sneaking away—but only until another "opportune time." (v.13)

Jesus had the strength to stare Satan in the eye and say, "No, I'm not going to do it in the way you are tempting me" because He had been faithful and loyal to God all of His life. He had learned about the nature of God in the Temple and in the synagogues. He had sung the Psalms, and He knew the meaning of scripture better than Satan who quoted them to Him. That may have been the first time, but certainly was not the last time, somebody looked at poetic language in the scripture and tried to test God to see if the literal metaphor was true. Jesus understood a deeper meaning of the sacred words which addresses the modern world as well as His ancient day. The Psalmist was not talking about arrows, stubbed toes, and protection from careless or stupid stunts. Jesus understood the protection, help, and comfort offered by God rested on the trusting of God rather than spectacular or miraculous works of men. Troubles, trials, and anxieties inflicted by life were best addressed by trusting God. (Of course this does not mean we ignore common sense activities to help ourselves.)

Our efforts, just as the efforts of Jesus, His disciples, and even Old Testament prophets, are not to be neglected; but they must be subjected to the ways of God. Living a life in which one believes God is present, in good times and bad, and with determination to always choose God's way rather than the dictates of Satanic forces, produces many benefits. In my age-stained study notes, I found reference to a Rabbi who said this Psalm teaches the world there is going to be an eternal Sabbath.

The key to the Psalm is found in the first and last verses. In the first verse, the picture is very clear. He who abides continually in the presence of God will be one who trusts God. Living and abiding with God as a continual relationship, not just at 11 a.m. on Sunday morning, but certainly at 11 a.m. on Sunday morning every blessed Sunday that you can, becomes a top priority. It is an experience that determines how the rest of the week is oriented.

The end of the Psalm, beginning at verse 14, is the voice of God making promises to those who dwell in His shelter because they "know my name." Here the Psalmist used the same concept the writer of Genesis used to describe Sarah, who, in an advanced age, "knew" her husband, Abraham, and conceived a child. To know God in this intimate personal way will guide all activities between Sunday worship and Saturday night bedtime. It will set our priorities, establish our values, encourage our spirits, and develop a spiritual maturity so that over a period of time we know that we know Him, and we know that He knows we know Him.

For the Christian, we must never be satisfied with revelation found in the Old Testament without testing it by the fuller revelation of the New Testament. We believe we have a truth foretold but not found in the Old Testament. True redemption and the everlasting refuge of which the Psalmist spoke are made possible by the resurrected Messiah, Jesus. The tomb opened and He came out. This is the action of God that fulfills the Psalmist's promise: "With long life I will satisfy them, and show them my salvation." (v.16) No earthly factor is more able to keep this assurance alive in our hearts than regular and devoted worship of God in fellowship with other believers. In a great oversimplification, we call it church, and Sunday is when it most often happens.

CHAPTER 9

GOD'S SHEPHERDING NATURE

Psalm 23

We can say with little doubt that Christians today, in our culture, make Psalm 23 the most frequently used, memorized, and referenced Psalm in Holy Scripture. We might even find that these are the most quoted words from the Bible. Their imagery, intimate nature, and religious sentiment have given support, hope, and comfort to every generation since the early days of the Old Testament. Though attributed to King David, they are rooted in the thought patterns of many other Old Testament characters that likened God to a shepherd. Elijah, Moses, and Amos all shared this same metaphor in explaining God's presence with Israel, both as a nation and as individuals.

Long before Jesus was born, Aristotle observed that music could convey the thoughts and feelings of people more completely than words alone. The marriage of music and poetry, as we experience it in the Psalms, reaches the deep recesses of the human psyche and expresses our innermost thoughts in profound ways exceeding our own expectations. This Psalm takes an almost childlike trust and applies it to our experiences, as a people and as individuals, in depths of emotion seldom encountered in other ways.

Poets have always expressed more than the surface of their words indicated. Truth spoken by the poet is often more profound than the words themselves. Every poet says more than the casual understanding of his or her words reveals. That's one reason their songs can be so repetitive. But it is an art in our society we don't usually appreciate. Seldom does anybody read poetry. That is our loss. But there are still

51

more than fifty courses related to poetry in the University of South
Florida catalogue. The poets, even though we think they aren't read,
still say more than we think they do.

Scholars have debated the precise event giving rise to the poetic
expression of Psalm 23. Some say it was David's experiences in caring
for his father's sheep on the hillsides of ancient Israel. He did this as
a lad and his great success in caring for the sheep led to him being
chosen to cast the stone at the giant Philistine, Goliath. Others say
the Psalm is based on David's experience when he and his friends
had to flee into the wilderness to avoid the warring conflict between
Jonathan and his father, King Saul. A few believe it is a Psalm of
trust based on some future event rather than a past one. Still others
say it is a pilgrimage Psalm based on the Exodus experience. It is
important to keep this point in mind when we observe that poets
often say more than we think they say. There are a number of words
in Psalm 23 that have no verb tense, as we understand it. These words
may be past tense, present tense, and future tense at the same time.
We do not have an English equivalent to this. Remember our earlier
observation, the poets often say more than we think they do.

In our Christian tradition we believe the New Testament is a fulfillment
of the Old Testament and superior to the Old Testament. It is fitting
to go to the New to find a fuller understanding of the Old, just as
we can often find a better understanding of the New by discovering
background data in the Old. Perhaps the best understanding of the
shepherd theme of Psalm 23 is found in John 10, where Jesus described
himself as the good shepherd.

In this gospel passage, the shepherd (1) is sensitive to the voice of
the sheep, recognizing each one individually. (vv.3-5,8,14,16,27) He
hears their needs and responds to each accordingly. The shepherd
(2) is unique and contrasted against the hireling or robber. (vv.1-2,8-
10,12-13) The shepherd (3) gives His life for His sheep. (vv.10-11,14-
15,17-18) The church calls this redemption, sacrificial atonement,
or Passion of Christ. The shepherd (4) gathers the wandering and
lost sheep into a single flock. (v.16) Here we understand the unity or
catholic nature of the church and the permanence of the Kingdom of

God. The sheep (5) have total security with the shepherd. (vv.28-29) Salvation is secured in Him.

The picture of Jesus being the good shepherd is one that will not die, because it is grounded firmly in the Old Testament imagery and expanded to maturity in the New Testament by the writers of the four gospels. The church has perpetuated this during the last two thousand years, and it has furnished one of the chief images of the clergy's job description. This in itself is one indication that the poet of the Psalter spoke more truth than he realized. This is also one reason the Psalm has endured and endeared itself to so many generations.

We can construct a variety of sermon themes using the concept of shepherd, banquets, valley of the shadow of death, anointing, rest, restoration, leadership of God, lack of fear, protection by God—on and on the list can go as it has for the past two millennia.

It will be helpful to look at the Psalm in what is perhaps the most ancient interpretation. This is done through what the most orthodox and liturgical traditions of our churches call the Sacraments of Initiation: Baptism, Chrismation (roughly equivalent to what many denominations call the communicants class), and the Lord's Supper.

Those who raise sheep in large quantity know they will not drink from "rough" water. It is the responsibility of the shepherd to find "still waters" (v.2) where the sheep can quench thirst and then "lie down in green pastures" (v.2) to rest, so digestion can take place. The ancient interpreters of this Psalm foresaw the baptismal font in this image of "still waters." Initiated into the faith, the experience of baptism provides our greatest nourishment, our greatest peace, and the place where we can find the greatest restoration. The Psalmist said more than he realized in this agricultural metaphor of "still waters."

Chrismation, the Orthodox concept roughly equal to the Protestant understanding of Confirmation, marks the coming of age of the baptized members of the church. The youth study hard. They make public their personal commitment to the Lord and Savior Jesus Christ. They begin to assume adult responsibilities in the faith community. In the Orthodox tradition—not ours—they are anointed with oil, a richly symbolic experience signifying commitment and personal outpouring of the Holy Spirit. The Psalmist said more than he realized when he declared, "You anoint my head with oil."

The latter part of the Psalm abandons the image of the shepherd in favor of the banquet. At the time this was written a person fleeing an enemy could seek refuge in the home of a stranger. If the stranger invited the fleeing person into his house, he was obligated to offer food and shelter. The pursuing enemy, by custom, was not allowed to take the fleeing party from the home where shelter and food had been offered. In the case of the Psalmist, the host prepared a banquet and had a great party while the enemy was left outside, looking through the window at the festivities. Some of the earliest New Testament interpreters saw in Psalm 23 a foreshadow of the Messianic Banquet, the Eucharist, Sacrament of the Lord's Supper. From the time Jesus sat with His disciples in the upper room until this day, the most sumptuous banquet of all, the one which saves us from the most threatening enemy of all, death itself, has been experienced at this Table. This is the best thing the shepherding God ever did for us. Again, the ancient poet said more than the words themselves meant.

(On the occasion of preaching this sermon, we observed the Sacrament of the Lord's Supper at this time. It was followed by the following commentary.)

In our day, it seems to me the greatest use of the 23rd Psalm is to bring comfort and affirm hope to those who are facing serious illness, injury, distress, or death. At these times we focus on walking "through the darkest valley" (v.4) and "I shall dwell in the house of the Lord my whole life long." (v.6) This is the greatest eternal promise we have, and it has been made possible because of the life, death, and resurrection of the Good Shepherd, Jesus Christ. The assurance from the Psalter has been put into effect by the life and work of the Messiah, Jesus of Nazareth. Today's poets are continually finding new ways to express this truth. Original tunes with slightly altered words may be set to new patterns of rhythm for a fresh expression of the ancient understanding of God's continual presence with His people.

A few years ago I heard one of these new compositions presented by its composer, John Michael Talbot, a Roman Catholic monk, who tours the world conducting spiritual renewal conferences and retreats. He sings and writes in the folk music style for the acoustic guitar. At the concert I attended, he explained the background of his musical interpretation of the 23rd Psalm in this manner. His father, a former Presbyterian Elder converted to Catholicism, was seriously ill in the Intensive Care Unit of an Indianapolis hospital. One evening he composed a new tune for the old words of the Psalmist and sang them, without accompaniment, as a prayer with his father. A few weeks later he composed a more complete musical arrangement for the guitar and sang it at his father's funeral. This popular songwriter and spiritual teacher had used his gifts and the poetry of the Psalter to pray a truth greater than the poet could imagine.

According to Matthew, those who observed the first Sacrament of the Lord's Supper sang a hymn following the meal and then departed. (26:30) A fitting way to conclude our worship is to meditatively listen to the new tune of the old words. Each of us can make this our prayer to find the assurance and hope promised in both the world's favorite Psalm and at this Table. In doing so, we are proclaiming the Lord's death until he comes again.

(Note: When this sermon was preached, a vocalist presented her interpretation of John Michael Talbot's musical offering described above. The first portion of the music was sung a capella. Toward the middle of the presentation an acoustic guitar joined her. Following the benediction the congregation was invited to remain for a time of personal quiet meditation. Those not wishing to remain for the period of meditation departed as quietly as possible.)

CHAPTER 10

CONFIDENCE

Psalm 63:1-8

I don't know how to fully account for it, but somewhere along the way, several years back, it became inappropriate in our culture and in most of our churches to express what in the Old Testament is known as prayers of lamentation. This is a common prayer theme in the Old Testament. Even one of the thirty-nine Old Testament books carries the name, Lamentations. For those who might need their memory refreshed, a lament is vocal, public crying out to God—or another person—in frustration, anger, sorrow, sadness, or confusion. These outcries are expressed because the speaker feels his or her life is not going very well at the moment. Life has been too severe. They have suffered unfairly or unjustly. They have to deal with difficulties and problems not of their own making. They have come from some place other than out of their own disobedience to God or human mistakes. Or maybe they just feel they have suffered enough.

The Psalmist was not plagued with a reluctance to express these feelings. To always think "positively" is not very realistic, and sometimes it is even unhealthy. Lament was so much a part of their life that 40% of the 150 Psalms dealt with this part of their existence. The habit of making lament known to God was allowable in Biblical days because the people of God believed God was always present. The exception to this belief would be that their sin had caused the departure of God. Even though God was not present at the moment, the prayers and offerings would eventually be heard, and God would return. God had assumed the responsibility and obligation to restore the former state of preferred status for Israel and its individual inhabitants. This was understood to be a part of the covenant relationship. It was the nature of God's steadfast love.

Generally these laments consist of: (1) words of praise for God, (2) a list of complaints with comparison to the former good times, (3) expression of confidence that God would make the requested changes, and (4) an invoking of some curse or doom upon the enemies of the person or nation speaking the prayer.

Tradition places the setting for Psalm 63 on the occasion of David's wandering in the wilderness to escape the deranged King Saul who was diligently searching for him. Should the King have his way, David would be executed. During this time of evading Saul, we can imagine David had difficulty finding accommodations, places of worship, food, and drink. These experiences provided a rich source of metaphors for David to describe his recollection of what a close relationship with God was like. According to the Psalm, the greatest loss David experienced during this period was his ability to worship according to his tradition within the community of God's people. Both the tone and specific words of the Psalm indicate the Psalmist desired fellowship with God in worship more than life itself. We can be sure he was concerned about his life. He was more concerned about fellowship with God.

We begin to see the depth of this concern in verse 1 as he speaks of his "thirst" for God. It is common knowledge that a human being can live only a short time without water. Thirst quickly comes upon us when we are cut off from this simple life supporting substance. Most of us drink every few hours. To be deprived of this for even a half-day produces a severe thirst. A full day without water leads to serious problems that quickly become life threatening. To "thirst" for God describes an intense unmet need. It is a revealing metaphor rooted in deprivation of a known benefit.

In God's sanctuary (which may or may not be a great temple or building, but is a place dedicated for communal worship) David had seen the power and glory of God. (v.2) He knew benefits derived from this encounter were more valuable than life itself. (v.3) Using another metaphor reflecting necessary human nourishment that might be sparse in the wilderness, the Psalmist equates knowing the presence of God with the satisfaction coming from a "rich feast." (v.5) Fine dining results in a mouth that praises. Following the feast, the Psalmist can go to bed, sleep soundly, and meditate—dream—about the joyous experience. (v.6) This nourishing fellowship results in the Psalmist clinging to God while recognizing God is continuing to hold him. (v.8)

It is the nature of God to hold on to His people, be they David, the Psalmist, all of Israel, or the reader of these words. This nature of God is described as *"hesed,"* translated in verse 3 as "steadfast love." It is perhaps the most mature and advanced understanding of God found in the Psalms. (This same concept is found in other places in the Psalms: 36:5, 89:14, and 107:1.) It generally means that God is reliable, helpful, and trustworthy. Those who depend on God can count on God's positive response to their needs. It is descriptive of the response the Old Testament prophet Hosea demonstrated to his wife Gomar even in her unfaithfulness to him. It is also a reminder of the New Testament words used to describe Jesus as the "pioneer" (Hebrews 2:10) who made our salvation possible because he came to "help." (Hebrews 2:18) A literal translation of the word is "run to our cry." The bedrock foundation of the word is trust. The one who trusts God does not depend on any other thing or any other self. Understanding this is a huge step forward in understanding the message and ministry of Jesus. We do not trust in order to attain the benefits of closeness to God—our own salvation. We trust purely because of God's nature. That was the Psalmist's thirst. He made his prayer with confidence that it would happen. God would again come and quench his thirst. He would again be able to lie on his bed at night and know God was holding him.

We seldom give great attention to the latter portion of the Psalm because it announces the Psalmist's assurance that those who are his enemies will be thoroughly destroyed. Their demise will be unquestioned—buried deep in the bowels of the earth, slain by the sword, bodies torn apart by jackals who devour the flesh and scatter the bones. (vv.9-10) As a result of this obliteration, "...the mouths of liars will be stopped." (v.11) These words are a reminder that the devil is described as a liar. (John 8:44) Even so, the tone of vengeance is out of character with the New Testament teaching of Jesus.

For the Christian we are again confronted with the need to read both the Old and New Testaments. It is the New that is the fulfillment of the Old. As wise and mature as the Psalmist was, he did not have all the answers. As much as Jesus could learn about God by singing these songs, He also brought us new and better insights into the one He most often called "Father."

As we ponder the situations that give us moments of lament, we can benefit from some of the teachings of Jesus found in the New Testament. Added to the insightful images of Psalm 63, these additional teachings can help us find even more peaceful rest on our bed and more delightful memories of the great feast prepared for us by the Son.

First, God is not an impartial observer of the happenings on earth and in our lives. The one whose immortality is beyond and above time is vitally concerned about our behavior within time. How else would He know whether or not a hair fell from your head? (Luke 21:18) Or why would the Son, Jesus, continue to pray to the Father, even in His final hours, if this were not true? (Matthew 27:46)

Second, God's judgment is the flip side of divine mercy, grace, and love, which would have no meaning if judgment did not exist. This judgment may not be in the manner we would choose or according to our standards, but God does hold us accountable. (John 5:19-30, Romans 2:1-11) This is a part of being in the covenant community.

Third, the fact that God takes sin seriously requires that we give it a great deal of attention as well. This will be a constantly perplexing situation for us. Already in this series we have identified several variations of sin described by Israel's musical poet. Missing the mark or getting lost is a very common way of understanding sin. At times our culpability is very personal due to our willful disobedience. On occasion it seems we harm only ourselves. Most often our behavior is injurious to our neighbors or faith community. These sins may be either known or unknown to us. At times they may be premeditated while others are impulsive. Some may become habitual while others are disobedient on some rare occasion. We cannot be comfortable or righteous when we adopt the attitude of "boys will be boys" and thereby tolerate behavior or attitudes contrary to the teaching of scripture. "White lies" are not acceptable, yet gray areas will always exist. Our response to sin must be condemning but with tact, restrictive but with mercy, informed but with prayer.

The fourth lesson is that vengeance belongs to the Lord and not us. "Vengeance is mine, I will repay, says the Lord." (Romans 12:19, Hebrews 10:30)

Finally, we must judge, when necessary, with caution. Mercy and grace are bedrock concepts guiding our relationships with others. Partial understanding of both God and humanity will always mark our finite and immortal nature. We have much in common with Jesus who admitted He did not have all answers to all things. (Matthew 24:36) We have even more in common with Paul who said his vision was "through a mirror, dimly." (1 Corinthians 13:12)

I find the passage from Romans to be of great help at this point. We have to make a wide variety of decisions related to these matters in daily life. Paul says that God's Spirit will be helping us in this process. He is praying for us. (Romans 8:26-27) This prayer is for both individuals and His church. We must be careful about casting the first stone. Jesus even directly told us not to do so. (John 8:7) The one who has come to give us salvation has instructed us in these matters. They can guide individuals, church congregations, religious hierarchies, and national political bodies.

When we pray about sin—*our* sin and *their* sin, whoever "*they*" are— God's spirit joins us even if we do not know it is happening. It is amazing how our vision clears. Our understanding becomes focused. Our trust in God's way grows stronger. And in the darkness of night we can, as the Psalmist said, lay on our bed and sleep well, for we are continually clinging to the God who is holding us. (Psalm 63:6-8) Our rest comes from God's steadfast love and power, rather than our work and worth. It is He who is the source of genuine confidence. Praise be to God!

CHAPTER 11

CONFESSION

Psalm 32 and Romans 4:1-8

A number of years ago the phone rang in the middle of a Saturday afternoon. It was an emergency. During the course of the remaining evening a plan was made. George, perhaps the most prominent lay leader of the church at that time, wanted to make a statement to the entire congregation on the following Sunday morning. He would be joined by his wife, who would probably not speak, and their two college age daughters who had been called home to join the family for this sudden and unforeseen occasion. After the sermon George and his family came to the chancel of the church. At floor level, with microphone in hand, and more than a thousand attentive listeners George confessed his adulterous relationship with a fellow employee. After his confession he sought the forgiveness of the congregation. His wife and daughters affirmed their offer of forgiveness and their determination to repair the family relationships. Circumstances of this affair would cause George to be terminated from his prominent position with a national retailer. He resigned all his positions within the church. George indicated they intended to remain in the church as members but employment opportunities, whatever they may be, would be key to determining where they would live.

During the next few weeks, I saw a church respond with greater love and support than could be imagined. The daughters were not ignored. A congregation learned in a new and fresh way the Christian response when sin has done its tragic deed. An entire church and a large part of the city experienced the Christian concepts of confession, forgiveness, repentance, redemption, and love to a degree greater than they were accustomed. It wasn't long until the president of another large retailer, an active churchman and one of George's main competitors for the past 20 years, offered George a job in another city at nearly the same level of responsibility. This was given with the assurance that he could expect appropriate promotions in the near future.

I cannot tell you the end of the story, but I can tell you that a few years later life was good for George and his family. He had progressed in his career. His daughters were happy. He and his wife were active in their church and each said their marriage was healthy and fulfilling.

George, his family, and his church had experienced at a deep and personal level the main teaching we can learn from Psalm 32. Whether this Psalm was written as a result of David's sin with Bathsheba, which is the traditional interpretation, or at some other date or occasion, we cannot know for sure. Scholars do agree, however, that it would be a fitting song to sing and celebrate how God dealt with David in that lustful, greedy, and selfish affair. It is also a fitting song to sing as one celebrates how God deals with any sin, adultery or not.

The Psalm begins with a description of the end-state of one that has confessed a long bottled-up sin within their own life and received the lovingkindness of God in forgiveness. The extensiveness and comprehensiveness of the forgiveness results in what we call a beatitude, as in the opening verses of the Sermon on the Mount. "Happy are those whose transgression is forgiven, whose sin is covered. Happy are those to whom the Lord imputes no iniquity, and in whose spirit there is no deceit." (vv.1-2) Some of the words used in these verses come from the financial world. The repentant sinner experiences God "covering" his sin as one would cover a bank overdraft. "Imputes," as used in verse two, describes the financial transaction in which one deposits money in the account of another. In this case the Psalmist is saying the Lord does not continue to place sin in the sinner's record. He has covered it by another means.

As is usually the case, the New Testament is a good commentary on the Old Testament. Paul uses these words from Psalm 32 in Romans 4 where he describes the work of Christ and the salvation offered by faith, not works. The New Testament usage comes out a bit differently because the translations move from Hebrew to Greek. Paul's words are "blessed is the one against whom the Lord will not reckon sin." (v.8) This covering of our sin was completed by the lovingkindness of God through the sacrifice of Jesus Christ. When we confess our sins, repent from them, and believe in the Lord's Son, our sins are covered and God quits depositing our sins in our account. The account has been fully covered—or settled—by Jesus. This is what the Passion of the Christ was about. This is what the Resurrection at Easter proved.

There is still more we can learn from the Psalm. Verses 3-6 are documentation of the poet's personal experience. The passage begins by describing the poet's internal agony, which is where God's conviction usually starts working in our lives. "While I kept silence, my body wasted away through my groaning all day long. For day and night your hand was heavy upon me; my strength was dried up as by the heat of summer."(vv.3-4)

This agony is followed by the key verse in the whole process. Here we must give our most careful attention to the Psalmist's words: "Then I acknowledged my sin to you, and I did not hide my iniquity; I said, 'I will confess my transgressions to the Lord,' and you forgave the guilt of my sin." (v.5) Do not be fooled at this point. Whether it is David of the Old Testament, George whom I told you about earlier, or the writer of these words, the confession must be specific. We must identify the sin we know about to God. He already knows it, but we have no way to "come clean" before God unless we are specific. We must, with God's help, also determine we will repeat the sin no more. The Bible calls this repentance. Confession without our determination to cease the action is bragging, not confession. Our temptation is to place most all our sins into some generic category, make a generic confession, and then continue our involvement with our preferred list. We must not continue to hold these preferred sins in some remote chamber of our heart or mind. Any sin we continue to cherish remains a barrier between God and us. Repentance has not been complete. Confession has not been total. Forgiveness will not come. The intimacy once known with God will be impossible.

We must not fall into the trap so often set by today's culture and made notable in recent weeks by several professional athletes. Sin is not a casual social blunder that can be erased by a half-hearted apology that ends with a defensive position explaining why we were justified in doing it. The four-year old whose parent says, "Tell your sister you are sorry you talked bad to her," is receiving good parental guidance. It is an inadequate response for a mature confession of sin. We have to look at our sin, see it as an offense to God, let it break our hearts as it does God's, and ask God's help to persevere in our determination never to do it again. This is the way we can experience the truth contained in 1 John 1:9, "If we confess our sins, he who is faithful and just will forgive us our sins and cleanse us from all unrighteousness." This is why he died for us. We must offer more than casual apologies and a promise to try harder to be better. Our dependence must be upon Him and our determination must be total.

The Psalm concludes (vv.6-10) with the poet's counsel for every one who has experienced this forgiveness of God to pray and join the congregation of the faithful. As a result, distress rushing at us like great floodwaters will not reach us. We can hide in the presence of God who will teach us the way we should go. He will always watch us so we must not be like the horse, quick to flee, or the mule, stubborn and resistive. The concluding picture in verse 11 is one we must not forget: "Be glad…rejoice…and shout for joy." This is difficult to do at the moment of confession—but it will come if confession is honest.

Though Romans 4 is a wonderful commentary on this passage, the parable in Luke's Gospel (15:11ff) is the best picture. The frequently told and beloved story is that of the younger son who was so unhappy in the father's house that he requested his share of the inheritance prior to the father's death. The social custom of the day could not have imagined a more humiliating request from a son. The father ignored the social custom and granted the son's wish. Over a period of time, the son, living in a far country and under conditions totally unacceptable in his own cultural background, agonized about his situation. Finally admitting he would be better off as a hired hand on his father's estate, he made preparation to return home. The son knew he would have to make confession to the father. The son also knew the entire village would know what he had done because his return would be very public.

The father in the story is the real surprise. Word of mouth traveled very fast in the villages of that day. Houses were close together. People were outside. People talked. The father knew his son was returning before the son could see his father. The father planned a banquet. Upon arrival at the home place, the greeting was joyous. Tears flowed. But the son had to confess—out loud—to the father. The sin had to be named. And then the party began. Joy, gladness, celebration! The elder brother, who had remained home performing the role of the eldest son faithfully but resentfully, refused to join in the celebration. He could not admit his sin of jealousy, his resentful nature due to the generosity of the father who had prematurely distributed the family's wealth and seen that portion evaporate into nothing. This fact had also cost him, the elder brother, a large sum because he had lost the benefit of capital appreciation over time. He would not confess. He would not repent. He could not be a part of the celebration.

Jesus learned from Old Testament experiences that forgiveness of sin depended upon confession and repentance. We learn from Jesus that it can only happen through our faith in Him. Then the celebration of glad rejoicing begins, for He has covered our sin, and it will not be deposited into our account again.

CHAPTER 12
FUTURE EXPECTATIONS

Psalms 126 and Philippians 3:4b-14

Across the years Psalm 126 has been among the least treasured and valued words in all scripture, perhaps even to the point of ridicule. Nevertheless, it is a wonderful opportunity to examine the basic attitude of God's faithful covenant community. It is this attitude we must examine and also look for a parallel in the New Testament.

Visualize the Psalm being sung as the people gathered for worship in the restored temple. The writer uses only past tense verbs for the first three verses. These first words cannot be underestimated, for it is here we discover the all important attitude, an attitude far more revealing than the words themselves would appear. "When the Lord restored the fortunes of Zion, we were like those who dream." (126:1) The great accomplishment of the past, deliverance from exile, and restoration of the temple resulted in a state of dreamlike ecstasy. As a result of God's past behavior, most any *present* could be endured because *past* experience created hope that would always be a *future* dream.

In rather different circumstances the apostle Paul demonstrated a similar attitude. Responding to a vision—some might call it a dream—he decided to go to Macedonia believing "that God had called (him) to proclaim the good news to them." (Acts 16:9ff) Not long afterwards he was jailed due to his preaching and the commotion it created in the community. Paul felt this treatment was improper since he had all the qualifications and stature the religious community might expect. He was properly initiated into the faith, from the right parentage, a practicing Pharisee, a zealous persecutor of the church, and never found to break any of the religious law. But when he became a follower of Jesus, these attainments became irrelevant. In fact, he said all these were "rubbish" (Philippians 3:5-8) and could be easily abandoned for the "righteousness from God based on faith" (v.9) in Christ. This was the dream Paul was following. He was committed to it, because he was able to remember what God had done for him on the Damascus road when he first responded to the work and word of Jesus. (Acts 9) The memory of his experience with Christ was never far from Paul's consciousness. Likewise, it was never far from his preaching which was always with "full conviction." (1 Thessalonians 1:5)

Both the Psalmist and Paul, as well as countless other believers throughout history, have had their lives so changed by the encounter with God that they could endure most any "present" affliction. Their ability to persevere during these trials was made possible by God and the dual focus on past and future rather than present. Neither the Psalmist nor Paul ignored the realities that must be dealt with in the present. At the same time both could hold on to a hopeful future due to the steadfast love of God they had experienced in the past.

One general technique to help understand the Psalms is to identify the speaker of the various lines in the poem. As you read a modern play, each speaking character is clearly displayed. This distinction is not so prominent in Old Testament poetry. Sometimes it is so confusing that experienced scholars disagree. However, we have no problem with this text. The Psalmist is the obvious speaker in verse 1 and the first part of verse 2. His nation, Israel, could also reaffirm his feeling using these exact words. The latter part of verse 2 reveals a change in speaker: "then it was said among the nations, 'The Lord has done great things for them.'" People who were not a part of the covenant could observe how God was blessing Israel. They could also observe the people's response to these blessings. As the nations of the world testified that God had blessed Israel, Israel readily agreed and rejoiced. (v.3) This was their declaration as they marched into the temple. Israel and the Psalmist were living a dreamlike existence of expectation based on past experiences with a loving and merciful God. Their trust had been born in the past but would be tested in the present.

The Psalmist, his nation, and all humanity encounters trouble in the present tense. At times it seems the present tense consists only of trouble. Missed field goals as time runs out, dysfunctional church members, business failures, down-sizing, rebellious children, unfaithful spouses, poor health, accidents, and earthquakes all contribute to present tense anxiety. Coping with such issues tends to fade in our memories. In the same manner the future seems so far away it is invisible.

The Psalmist did not allow present difficulties to erode his memory or erase his hope. The latter half of the Psalm is his prayerful testimony. In the Old Testament we often find that planting the crop and grief are related concepts, whereas harvest and joy are at the opposite end of experience. This agricultural experience provided the necessary images to convey his attitude of full conviction. It was his prayer that the "watercourses" in the Negev (desert) would again flow with life-giving nourishment. (v.4) Food and prosperity would abound. His prayer becomes very picturesque: "May those who sow in tears reap with shouts of joy. Those who go out weeping, bearing the seed for sowing, shall come home with shouts of joy, carrying their sheaves." (vv.6-7) There is no lack of confidence here. The future will be better. The God of steadfast love will answer this prayer.

It is this same conviction—this same memory of the former works of God—which allowed Jesus to cope with his anxiety at Gethsemane just prior to the crucifixion. His past experience with God overshadowed the present difficulties and gave him a future hope. It is difficult to think Jesus did not have this attitude partially developed by singing this Psalm as a youth. Even in this dark hour he could trust God with hope. Likewise, it is not difficult to imagine Paul, confined to prison, recalling this same Psalm as he wrote, "forgetting what lies behind and straining forward to what lies ahead, I press on toward the goal for the prize of the heavenly call of God in Christ Jesus. Only let us hold fast to what we have attained." (Philippians 3:13-16) Here Paul chose to release the memory of persecution. He chose to remember the more remote past to fuel his hope for the future. He would "press on."

It has been almost exactly 50 years since two athletic events caught my attention. One happened to me as I was hanging around the track where my high school track coach was holding practice. I was not on the team nor could I have ever hoped to be. I was surprised when the coach called me over to where the team was practicing. They wanted to run a competitive mile relay but had only 7 team members available. He recruited me to be the 8th person. With about 20 seconds of instruction he set me up to run the second leg of the mile relay. I stumbled and fell badly skinning my knee on the cinder track. My team lost. The second event was Roger Bannister running a mile in less than four minutes. A task once considered impossible and perhaps destructive to the human body, should it be accomplished, was headline news around the world. A mile run in less than four minutes!! After months of agonizing training—most of it during his medical school lunch hour—he broke a world record many said was humanly impossible. In my only effort at track and field events, I received 20 seconds of instruction and crashed to the ground at least 50 yards short of a 440 yard goal. Which one of us "pressed on" (Philippians 3:14) in the manner described by Paul? Which of us demonstrated commitment to the event? Which one did the nations of the world watch?

The prophet Isaiah declared that Israel would be a "light to the nations." (Isaiah 49:6, 60:3) The implication of this prophecy is that the light would attract the nations to Israel as they observe the blessings God put upon them. It is not so clear that Israel should become aggressive in taking that light to the nations. There is a difference between placing a light where it may be seen should one happen to pass by as opposed to making sure the path is kept clear so the possessor of the light can take it to those who may pass by. One is passive while the other is active. The passive position of the Psalmist reaped results. The nations said, "The Lord has done great things for them." (v.2)

We should note the contrast between the basic positions of the Old Testament and the New Testament positions of Jesus (Matthew 28:18-20) and Paul (Acts 16:11-16) on this issue. The New Testament is much more aggressive. When Jesus came as a light to the nations (John 1:4ff) it was a bold and assertive invasion into the world. We should not be surprised that He instructed His disciples to live in the same manner. Nor should we be surprised that this lifestyle would create "present tense" problems. We can find comfort and guidance in the writing of the Psalm and Paul, plus the words of Jesus, as we keep the dual focus on what God has done for us and what has been promised to us.

Meanwhile, in the present age, we can march regularly to the houses of worship and let the nations observe our praises to God. We can proclaim great thanksgivings for the bounty placed upon us by a generous Father. We can let the nations hear our prayers, even the prayers we offer on their behalf.

We do these things—things the Psalmist did—knowing the nations are watching, but we should solve a few problems. First, we tend to confuse—perhaps ignore—the difference between a personal testimony and the testimony of the group. We err by choosing one and eliminating the other. The nations are watching the group <u>and</u> the individuals. Both have important testimony to give. I, like Paul and you, must continue to "press on" as I deal with present problems. I can stand firm and move forward, with one foot rooted in my past experience with God and the other placed on the firm foundation of the risen Lord and His promises for the future.

Another problem we face is giving proper attention to the individual testimony we can make to the "nations" we touch. These are the ones who sleep in our homes, work with us, participate in our neighborhood watch, belong to our clubs, sit beside us on church pews, and cheer with us in athletic stadiums. Rather than just letting them watch us, we have opportunities to give an explanation. The story needs to be simple, as it was with the Psalmist, who declared "the Lord has done great things for us." (v.3) It also needs to be "present tense" as it was with Paul who wrote amidst the suffering of prison life, "I press on toward the goal." (Philippians 3:14)

The words of the Psalmist, the writings of Paul, and the teachings of Jesus merge to give us a final picture of our future expectations. Trust built on what God has done in the *past* delivers us from undue guilt. Expectations presented to us from these three streams of spiritual nourishment provide us *future* hope even in the greatest of difficulties. *Present* anxiety is fleeting. Praise God, "The Lord has done great things for us." (v.3) Pray for the nations to be watching. Amen.

CHAPTER 13

THE CLEANSING NATURE OF

WORSHIP

Psalm 118 and Philippians 2:5-11

From the age of 12 until I was ordained as a minister I maintained church membership in the same congregation. During that time I suppose at least 95% of the Sunday worship services began with the pastor speaking these words: "This is the day that the Lord has made; let us rejoice and be glad in it." (Psalm 118:24) This greeting from Psalm 118, used by the pastor of my youth, has been in my memory bank for more than a half century. Very likely the Jewish community used some of these same words as they assembled for worship or some holy day celebration during the days of young Jesus. They were a part of the standard liturgy of ancient Israel. We can expect they made an impression on Jesus just as they made an impression on me. After all, the scripture tells us that He worshiped regularly just as I did. (Luke 4:16) He would have heard them sung or spoken, in unison or antiphonal response, perhaps as a solo voice or group. They would have embedded themselves within His mind just as they did mine.

This Psalm presents the voices of the priests, king, worship leaders and congregation assembling for the purpose of worship. Each of these gives witness to how God has guided, protected, and nurtured them in their life experiences. Remembering these characteristics of God, they gather to honor and praise Him. The author of this Psalm sandwiches the entire prayerful testimony between the recurring theme, "Give thanks to the Lord, for he is good, for his steadfast love endures for ever." (vv.1,29) These words, regularly sung, had to have been a part of the educational experience of Jesus. Surely they would have nurtured Him as they do us.

During the days of the New Testament, the Christian community made some changes in their worship patterns from that of their Jewish ancestors. The driving force to these changes was the resurrection of Jesus. Since God raised Him on the first day of the week, the Church chose to worship Him on that day. We remember it weekly on Sunday, the day of Christian worship, and annually with Easter. Truly, this was the day the Lord made. None other has ever been like it.

I have heard that Martin Luther called this his favorite Psalm. As one of the key leaders of what we call the Protestant Reformation—some people would call him *the* leader—he found himself at odds with the Pope, Bishops, King, and most of the religious and civil bureaucracy of his day. This is the kind of Psalm that would bring a man under extreme pressure much comfort. The Psalmist's conviction that God would always be present with him—if not now then surely soon—would be reassuring. Praying these words over and over in both public and private worship would result in a sense of cleansing, refreshment, and nurturing. Sins would be forgiven. Spirits would be lifted. Renewal would be experienced. Luther would leave the worship experience with more hope than he had upon arrival, just as did the Psalmist. That would be a really good thing. Even better, the same cleansing experience can happen for us.

When Jesus came, He discovered some things had gone wrong with worship in His day. As He approached the temple during Holy Week, He encountered persons taking unfair advantage of others in financial transactions. Some were selling inferior sacrificial animals to pilgrims who had come great distances to worship. Perhaps others were charging too much or taking advantage by making unfair or unethical currency exchanges. This is why He chased them out of the Temple. "But," you say, "how did He know they were unfair?" To paraphrase Paul, "He used to live in heaven, you know—with the Father." We also are certain He would have learned the system by just living in the area for 30 years.

The Philippian passage for the day explains all this by the wonderful expression, "he emptied himself." (2:7) He did not want to hold on to what He had in the heavenly home with the Father. He was compassionate and willing to act on that compassion. His love for the world—a world gone wrong—caused Him to become like us: to walk in our shoes, experience our human form, know our human temptations, and live our daily sufferings even to the point of death. (vv.7-8) In this "emptying" of Himself, He revealed to us down here what life could be like up there. He learned what life was like down here, so He could prepare the way for us to be up there. (Note: I do not believe in the ancient concept of a three-tiered universe. Perhaps I should have said: "beyond time and space of the material cosmos" for "up" and "within time and space of the material cosmos" for "down." Most people understand the simpler expression, though.)

One of the difficulties we have in understanding what Jesus did for us is that we tend to be very much like each other. We even cultivate ways to be with people who are like us. Most of us don't search for ways to be with those who are different from us. Even when we make the effort to be with or understand those who are different, we don't usually go to the far extreme.

Shortly after moving to Tampa in 1978, I met Ophelia. We worked in the same office and became very good friends. The friendship lasted far longer than our working relationship and ended with her death about nine years ago. She was several years older than I and came to this country when Castro gained control of Cuba. When she arrived in New York along with several of her immediate family, she had no material possessions, only the clothes she was wearing. There was a serious financial struggle for her and the rest of her family members. One of her gifts was the ability to tell a good story. As our acquaintance grew into friendship, we learned much about each other. It did not take long for me to realize she came from a background of wealth I could not even imagine. For instance, until arriving in this country, she did not know that a bar of soap got smaller as it was used. In her home the maid replaced each bar after it had been used once. She never saw a bar of soap that had been used. If she happened to sit on her bed or just lie down for a brief moment, the maid changed the sheets. She and her husband took a honeymoon that lasted two and a half years. Accompanied by a maid and a butler, they visited every country in the world except Guam. What a honeymoon! Financially and socially, the distance traveled as a refugee from where she was reared to the streets of New York was greater than I can imagine. But it was nothing compared to the distance Jesus traveled from heavenly existence to the form of a servant in Israel so He could be the High Priest making atonement for our sins. (Hebrews 2)

During the last few weeks, our nation has been inundated with promotion, publicity, advertising, and discussion about Mel Gibson's movie, "The Passion of the Christ." I confess I have not seen it, but I plan to do so in the future. In the meanwhile, I have probably read or seen on television at least 75 discussions related to the subject. Much, if not most, of them are concerned in some way with *who* killed Him. I can understand this concern in the context of anti-Semitic issues. Quite frankly, the church made a grievous error of prejudice and theology a long time ago when they focused on *who* did the deed. For the Christian it is not a very important question. The vital issues are *why* He was killed and *who* He was. These questions were not fully answered until the Easter morning resurrection.

I have been able to identify more that 40 terms in the Bible used to describe *who* He was: man, God, son of David, savior, prophet, stone, bridegroom, judge, lamb, scapegoat, mediator, messiah, king, high priest, and lord are just a few. He was God dwelling with us in human form, fully God and fully man. We have to live with the resulting paradox. We will be woefully deficient if we make Him just a good teacher or a significant philosopher. And, certainly, He was more than a myth.

Why He was killed is an equally challenging and important question. Again, many Biblical words and phrases are used to help form an answer to this query. To save us from sin, to redeem us, to make the sacrifice acceptable to God, and to reveal the best picture we can have of God are a few of the many ways to answer the question of *why* He came. Each one is only a partial answer. From the ancient story of Abraham until the resurrection morning, the teaching of scripture is that God would use an agent to bring fulfillment of the covenant promise rather than geography. Many people helped in the process, but it was not completed until Jesus, God's own Son, became that agent, the promised Messiah. It was He who came, suffered, died, and was resurrected that life as God intended could be present now and eternally.

We will miss the meaning of Lent, Holy Week, and Easter if we do not realize the entire experience of the passion of Jesus was a deliberate and voluntary action. Frequently, when things are not going so good, the coach or CEO voluntarily or under a great deal of pressure "steps down." Seldom, if ever, is this expression used to describe the retirement, job change, or promotion of a person at a time of their voluntary choice. It is always associated with a demotion or termination under pressure.

Jesus did not just "step down" from the Father's presence. He "emptied himself taking the form of a slave, being born in human likeness... and became obedient to the point of death—even death on a cross." (Philippians 2:7-8) This was a voluntary action rooted in the love of God for all creation. It was the culmination of the thought repeatedly expressed by the Psalmist as he processed to the temple for worship: "O give thanks to the Lord, for he is good; his steadfast love endures for ever!" (vv.1,3,4,29)

Leaving all that He had, Jesus became all that we are—but without sin—in order that we could become what God intended at the moment of creation. When the experiences of that first Holy Week were over, the followers of Jesus knew God had done something that was unrepeatable. There was the beginning of a new focus in their worship. Today we continue in that same tradition. Our liturgy—the work of the people— is but another step along the path made clear by others. We set our eyes on Jesus, *who* He was and *why* He did what He did, and we worship. We are cleansed, washed whiter than snow (Isaiah 1:18), forgiven, and made new. We discover, as did the Psalmist, that "the Lord is (our) strength and (our) might; he has become (our) salvation." (v.14)

These words, as Jesus sang them in the days of His youth, must have given Him great hope. Perhaps He had some foresight as to how much hope they would give us. "This is the day that the Lord has made; let us rejoice and be glad in it." (v.24)

CHAPTER 14

STARTING OVER

Psalm 118:1-2, 14-24, Isaiah 28:16, and Luke 24:1-12

A few weeks ago Richard Clarke, a long time civil servant, published a book outlining what the Bush administration knew, who knew it, and when they learned it concerning weapons of mass destruction in Iraq. It did not take long before an official of the Bush administration said that if Clarke's book was correct, it undermined the very cornerstone of his own argument. I do not cite this raging national mass media debate to make a political statement. I use it only to focus our attention on the word "cornerstone." We have encountered more frequent use of this word on a local basis to describe the error of the Tampa Bay Buccaneers in trading away defensive end Warren Sapp. It is used even more abundantly to describe the failure to re-sign safety John Lynch. Surely the team will fall apart because the cornerstones are gone. Again, I am not here to give advice to the Bucs, although I am sure they could benefit from my thoughts on the matter.

I do not know where or when the use of cornerstone as a metaphor began. The Jewish community seems to have used it for about 3,000 years. In the Old Testament sometimes the cornerstone image is used to represent God. At other times it refers to the temple or community of Israel. On occasion, it is the top cap of a wall. In the Isaiah passage, it is a messianic image standing for the stability, strength, and foundation of faith. This seems to be the primary meaning and is dependent upon understanding the construction process. The cornerstone was carefully selected because of its size, perfection, and strength. Usually the first part of the construction, it was used as the foundation point of two walls. If it had been well chosen and positioned, it would give great strength to two walls rather than one. The building would be more difficult to destroy. In addition, it would furnish a permanent reference point for the rest of the construction. Place a door 20 paces from the cornerstone. Turn the wall in a new direction at 27 paces. The Christian community borrowed this thought from Isaiah, and every time it is used in the New Testament it is a direct reference to Jesus as Messiah. The concept was even broadened by Paul in his letter to Ephesus where he indicated the disciples and apostles who built on the cornerstone would take on the characteristics of the cornerstone. (Ephesians 2:20-22)

One of the more interesting parts of the story of the Passion is the burial of Jesus. The Son of God, who had no place to lay His head, came to rest in a tomb owned by Joseph of Arimathaea. Evidently Joseph was a man of wealth. His burial plot was a hillside cave, as opposed to the town dump. Being entombed in the cave, the body would have been properly prepared, wrapped and anointed with spices to help control the odor. A fitted stone would then be placed at the door of the cave. This would prevent wild animals from entering and scattering either flesh or bones. In the case of Jesus, there was no time to prepare the body before burial, which must be accomplished prior to sundown. The women, after proper Sabbath observance, were still concerned about the lack of full and proper preparation for the burial and went to the tomb early the next morning to complete the process. This is when they discovered the stone door had rolled away and the cornerstone had rolled out. (This phrase is used with no disrespect intended. When I first used it, an elder of the church came to me afterwards and remarked that I should have added even one more phrase: "The stone door rolled away, the corner stone rolled out, now let the good times roll.")

A few years ago I heard Emily Chandler at a denominational workshop tell about a conversation she had with her granddaughter, whom I believe she said was 5 years old. It went something like this: "Grandma, did you know some bad men killed Jesus?" "Yes." "Did you know they put him on a cross?" "Yes." "Did you know they buried him?" "Yes." "But Grandma, did you know he got up?!!" The little girl understood the essence of Easter and our Christian faith. The door rolled away. The cornerstone rolled out.

The prophecy of Isaiah had been fulfilled. The vision of the Psalmist had come to pass. The one who was to be the foundation of our faith got up. The stabilizing influence in times of confusion, the place where we could get our bearings and visions for the journey ahead, was still alive. The source of our values for now and eternity—the cornerstone for all this and more—could not be contained in the grave. Death itself could not break the cornerstone.

When persons discuss or compare religion and science, the bodily resurrection of Jesus usually finds itself on the agenda. The difficulty arises when science wants to explain religion using scientific methodology. The same problem exists for religion wanting to explain science using the religious frame of reference. Religion needs to admit there is no scientific—perhaps we should say natural—way to explain the existence of life after death. This issue is a matter of religious faith and is not unusual for persons of religious belief. By faith we believe God exists and is the creator. It is also faith that produces the conviction that time is linear and history is going somewhere. Likewise, by faith we believe God is still involved in creation. We have little problem in believing God will not allow death, as we know it, to be the end of all things. Those of us who walk around on this earth, as well as the earth upon which we walk, and the cosmos in which it floats, will eventually die. For us it usually happens in our seventh decade. For the cosmos, it may be billions of years away. Even science agrees that it will come to an end in some manner, in spite of the present vigor and aliveness. God, who has both will and purpose, will not allow human or cosmic death to defeat His purpose. This conviction is fundamentally a religious faith, based on the nature of God and demonstrated by the resurrection of Jesus. There is a destiny for us beyond time and space.

A Biblical description of this new creation is found in Revelation 21. "Then I saw a new heaven and a new earth; for the first heaven and the first earth had passed away, and the sea was no more. And I saw the holy city, the new Jerusalem, coming down out of heaven from God, prepared as a bride adorned for her husband. And I heard a loud voice from the throne saying…'Death will be no more, mourning and crying and pain will be no more, for the first things have passed away.'" (v.1ff) The covenant community of God's people has a destiny after this one.

The cornerstone rolling out of the grave furnishes for us the way of eternal hope. Yet the Easter experience is not so much about us, as it is about God. It is in Easter that we learn about God in the most dramatic fashion. Here we see most clearly why God allowed His Son to come to this earth. Here we experience God raising Him from the dead. (Romans 8:11) In the resurrection we know God as one "who gives life to the dead and calls into existence the things that do not exist." (Romans 4:17) In the process of making "life from the dead" (Romans 11:15) we know the lovingkindness of God multiplied by infinity.

When we come to know God like this, we soon discover how the Easter experience is about us. We are not just specks on earth. We are not just a blip in the evolutionary process. Created in His image, we are children of God, determined by God to be worthy of mercy and redemption for something better. History, which is moving toward God, has a place for us. "By his great mercy he has given us a new birth into a living hope through the resurrection of Jesus Christ from the dead." (1 Peter 1:3)

Easter is first about God, then about us. It is also about our task on earth. If we, who build our foundation on the cornerstone of Jesus, are also expected to take on the characteristics of that same cornerstone, we have something to do in this life. We have responsibility to add to what God is building. The resurrection from which we get life also provides a purpose for our lives. The result of the Easter experience is so grand, so good, and so life-giving we are compelled to tell the story. The women who first discovered the tomb to be empty furnish an eternal example of going to tell somebody what has happened rather than sitting on the secret. The tale had to be told.

No matter how we look at the Easter experience, we recognize it carries with it an understanding that we can have another chance in life. In the last few years I have seen two interesting phrases in religious writing, but I do not know who first used the expressions. I think they have become very common in religious circles. The first is, "We are an Easter people living in a Good Friday world." Suffering, prejudice, injustice, selfishness, and terror are all around us. On a daily basis we deal with the seeds of evil that produced what we call Good Friday. There is always somebody trying to get Jesus out of the way. The second expression is "don't let Easter become a second-hand experience." It is personal and needs to be individual. Each of us must follow the path of Mary, Joanna, the unnamed women, and the disciples they brought to the empty tomb. Though we cannot see the physical place of emptiness on the Jerusalem hillside, we can feel the emptiness in our lives. We need another chance. We need to start over. We need another beginning.

Jesus, the cornerstone, gave us a wonderful parable about construction that has worked its way into the common language of our world. "Everyone then who hears these words of mine and acts on them will be like a wise man who built his house on rock. The rain fell, the floods came, and the winds blew and beat on that house, but it did not fall, because it had been founded on rock. And everyone who hears these words of mine and does not act on them will be like a foolish man who built his house on sand. The rain fell, the floods came, and the winds blew and beat against that house, and it fell—and great was its fall." (Matthew 7:24-27)

As a boy, and later in early adulthood, Jesus sang the Psalm about a promised cornerstone. The prophecies of Isaiah were embedded in His mind. In the garden just prior to the crucifixion, He wondered why this was happening. On Easter morning, He knew the answer. God was starting over and all who make Him Lord can be a part of what God is doing.

As long as you can hear this message, you have a chance to build on a different foundation. You can start over. Let it be the cornerstone, the one who rolled out on Easter morning, who furnishes the proper foundation. Go and tell this to the world. The cornerstone is still here.

CHAPTER 15

FRIENDS

Psalm 55 and John 15:12-15

Every one of us has experienced the treachery of a friend. It may have been a friend who stole money, a precious keepsake, or perhaps a good reputation. Some of our friends have been known to go after our spouses. Others betrayed a confidence and turned it into gossip. Sometimes a friend inflicts child abuse, rape, or murder. Friends have even turned into spies for an enemy country. Occasionally, even the clergy friend will commit an act of betrayal, and entire congregations are seriously wounded.

Our Psalm today focuses upon just one narrow aspect of friendship, but I am sure it is an aspect we have all tasted. Keep in mind I am not talking about a casual acquaintance or somebody you have to work with at the office or factory. I'm not even talking about a teammate. The friend the Psalmist was concerned about was a best buddy. Their relationship was true intimacy, but not sexual. Webster's Dictionary describes a friendship as: marked with respect; a regard for liking; neither intimate nor wholly dependent on business or professional ties; one who knows all about us but is loyal to us just the same.

Not long ago, while having lunch with one of my friends in another city, he described an experience he and his wife had the previous evening with another couple. The four of them had gotten together at his house for dinner, the purpose of which was to discuss a common business interest. The evening went along according to plans, but the guests lingered too long, and, as described by the host, they may have had a bit too much wine. Eventually the guests began the departing ritual, shook hands vigorously, embraced their hosts enthusiastically, and declared, "This has been a really fabulous evening. We have bonded so well. I know we will be friends forever." My friend said to me, "The idiot didn't know you can't make a friend in one evening. That takes years, if ever." The "if ever" is very important in this discussion. Most of us have very few friends. In fact, Gale Sheehy, in her best selling book, Passages, indicated one is particularly blessed if they have three really good friends. Some will say the more acquaintances we have, the fewer friends we have—there just isn't time. Maybe some of us make many acquaintances as a way of avoiding a deep, intense friendship. A recent Parade magazine article indicated TV personality Bill O'Riley would probably agree with my friend and Ms. Sheehy that real friends, rather than acquaintances, are rare.

It is also why one person wrote a note, which in reality was his last words: "I am going to walk across the city to the bridge and if one person looks me in the eye or smiles I will not jump."

The Psalmist was depressed that his friend—his best friend—much more than an acquaintance, teammate, or colleague at work, had betrayed him. This betrayal, more than any other circumstance, triggered his heartfelt lament. This particular Psalm is one of more than 40 we put in the lament category, by far the largest single category within the entire collection of 150. Some are intensely personal, while others are obviously national in nature. They were based on Israel's idea that God was present in their life and that they could converse with Him about anything, good or bad. Placing any complaint one had before God, the Psalmist believed, was appropriate and normal behavior. God would then do what He willed, but the Psalmist was sure his prayers, vindictive as they may be, would be heard. God would be as open to his prayers as any human friend would be open to his conversation. In this sense, God was the bartender hearing whatever complaints one desired to express.

The Psalmist's reaction to the betrayal by his intimate friend provides all generations a guide for handling these gut wrenching and too common experiences. Psalm 55 is the work of a man in great distress and anxiety. Experiencing troubles crashing down on him from all sides, his greatest disappointment was the betrayal of the friend with whom he had broken bread and worshipped on many occasions. Human treachery was displaying its most insidious behavior. His first reaction has been replicated in perhaps every one of our lives. Run away, hide, deny, avoid the hurt, and don't face the embarrassment. (vv.6,8,12) Yet the Psalmist was clinging to his hope placed in a sovereign God, much as one wrecked at sea clings to the only floating object he can find. With an eye on towering waves, his ear in tune with raging winds, and fearful of what must be swimming in the water around him, his prayer of lament went out to God: "Lord, bring a curse down upon him. Take his life." (v.15)

Even though the negative feelings were real, the Psalmist knew he would get through the pain of disappointment. Even in this very human relationship, he could depend on God to supply the help he needed for God would not "permit the righteous to be moved." (v.22)

Today, due to our life experiences, most of us can feel our kinship with the Psalmist. Yet, at a deeper gut level, the Psalmist knew the behavior of his friend—and others—had nothing to do with the Psalmist's relationship to God. The actions of friends are not, and must not be, the determinative factors in how we live with God. Our friends may disappoint us and we may disappoint our friends, but God is not in the "disappointing" business. Trust placed in the Lord is trust placed where it should be. It is our only secure depository.

The best place to see how this plays out in life is to look at Jesus. A part of the function of His incarnation was to show us how to live in relationship with each other and the Father.

The text from John's Gospel tells us that He called His disciples His friends, and Judas was among them. Then he reminded His friends—or disciples—that the greatest gift was love, which would cause one to lay down his life for another. He went on to remind them that a friend of the world was not a friend of God. And Judas was there.

As Jesus sang and prayed the Psalms in the days of His youth, He was immersed in the Hebrew religious culture that taught Him God was always present. Occasionally, some in Israel might think God was hiding, or that they could flee to some remote place where God could not reach them. Jonah tried to run away from God. Even Jesus, in his darkest moment, wondered why the Father had abandoned Him. Yet they still prayed, indicating some kind of belief that God was close enough to hear.

From being exposed to the Psalms in early childhood, Jesus could also learn that there would be a variety of choices before Him. He could "follow the advice of the wicked" (Psalm 1:1) or He could follow the "way of the righteous." (Psalm 1:6) In His adult years, Jesus identified this idea as the "narrow" contrasted with the "broad" roads—one headed for life, the other for destruction. (Matthew 7:13-14)

With respect to our friends in this day, the same world view described above is present. The ancient message is still true. God is with you, even when you are with your friends. Choose carefully, as did Jesus, and learn from Him.

Jesus chose His friends, His disciples, but He did not let them determine His strategies. He enjoyed, and indeed valued, their relationships, but He did not let them determine how He would do His work. He knew, as did the Psalmist, the possible treachery of friendships. Judas was there.

Jesus did not abandon His friends. He is not the one who left the room. Even as He went to the cross, He was doing it for His friends.

Jesus did not depend ultimately on His friends. He did not find His self-worth based on a peer group at school. He did not find His self-image determined by how well He was liked at work. He did not get His ego lifted by knowing and being friends with prominent people. He did not even leave His "church" when His friends sinned.

Jesus did not let His friends determine His values. Though Jesus was criticized for eating with the sinners, He was never criticized for adopting their lifestyle, habits, values, or attitudes. He was a friend strong enough to change them, rather than letting them change Him.

Jesus still desired the relationship of friends. Too often we ignore these words Jesus said directly to His disciples: "You are my friends if you do what I command you. I do not call you servants any longer, because the servant does not know what the master is doing; but I have called you friends, because I have made known to you everything that I have heard from my Father." (John 15:14-15) Christians of today must not forget we are now placed in the "friend of…" category of Jesus. We will be tempted to betray Him. We must not yield.

It is much better to learn the nature of true friendship from Jesus and the Psalmist than to learn from "Friends," a canceled TV sit-com. Though it was a popular show for several years, can you imagine what your life would be like if you were in that group? There was not enough integrity among the whole bunch to fill a teaspoon. Their silliness and buffoonery could make us laugh, but somebody was always trying to take advantage of or manipulate somebody else.

Both the Psalmist and Jesus could survive the betrayal of their friend because each was grounded in a personal relationship with God. Though they wanted and enjoyed friends, their faith, their values, and their lifestyle came from another source. Borrowing an image used in the previous chapter, their friends might be bricks in their wall, but they had a different cornerstone. Both Jesus and the Psalmist knew their friends made a joyous contribution to their life, but there was always the possibility of treachery, betrayal, and failure.

As valuable as earthly friends are, it is more important to build your life on the cornerstone of Jesus who, as a youth, learned to sing and pray to God, "I will trust in you." (v.23)

CHAPTER 16

PRAISE

Psalm 150 and Revelation 1:4-8

What is the most important thing a person can do? This was the question several seminary students discussed late one evening in the dormitory lounge. It is a relevant question for anyone, seminary student or not. Answers will depend on a variety of factors. For example, does "do" include something which would be primarily "thought" as opposed to "action?" What does "important" mean? Breathing is important and so is procreation. Are we evaluating this sort of action? In spite of how we might answer the question, I am sure that most of the Psalmists' contemporaries would have answered, "Praise God." Giving praise to God is the kind of worship experience the Old Testament assumes covenant people will practice, both publicly and privately. It is the most important action one can do purely because of who and what God is. Nothing else can be compared to God.

This belief in the supremacy of God led Israel to develop a wide range of words to explain various ways this praise can be accomplished. The most important of these is translated "hallelujah" or "praise." It is a verb that involves action rather than passive thought and is based on the nature of God rather than the work or deeds of God. When we move to praising God because of what has been done, we are moving into thanksgiving for specific actions. This is praising because we have benefited in some way. The experience is not as pure as praise/hallelujah without regard to any of God's actions. Other words used to explain the praise and worship of God are glory, renown, sing, shout, rejoice, bless, and thanks. I am sure I have not exhausted the list.

They all are a bit short of the most important concept of hallelujah/ praise. It all starts with the recognition of God's supremacy over everything else. We praise God—hallelujah—because of God's nature.

Psalm 150 is a fitting conclusion to the Psalter and this sermon series. Visualize the congregation of Israel beginning to assemble at the temple for their weekly worship. Visualize our congregation, as we have just done, assembling at the church building for our weekly worship. Here, as well as in Biblical times, there are actions associated with the praise of God that are important enough to stand apart from the strict concept of praise. Some of them are fasting, preaching (utterances), meditation, offerings, and making sacrifices. In this Psalm our attention is most specifically focused on praise. We begin our praise and encounter the Spirit of God as we greet each other with hospitality. We praise God and the nations watch. These nations see lives being changed because of what happens to those who praise God. We call it salvation. And all of us rejoice that brokenhearted, dispirited, and lonely persons are made whole. We call it ministry; healing; miracle; work of God.

A careful study of the Psalms will disclose six aspects of communal and private praise of God. Each, to some degree, is found in the few words of Psalm 150. Keep in mind that Jesus learned about this when He sang these very same words. First, *whom* shall we worship? Already we have devoted much attention to the answer of this question. Every line of the poem contains the admonition to praise the Lord. Note the psalm does not mention this kind of praise being placed upon nation, king, spouse, family, children, money, awards, applause, fame, or accomplishment. Nothing else is worthy of this praise. With God as the object of our praise, we worship to give, not to get. The idea that we must "get something out of it" is an immature understanding of what happens when we praise God. We do not worship with the same expectation we have when we make a department store purchase or pay a fee to attend a sporting event. It is a pure gift to God.

I think I was a young adult before I fully understood this act of giving praise to God with zero expectation. I have always enjoyed music. I took lessons as a child. I played in high school orchestra and sang in school and church choruses. During my second year of seminary I listened to the male chorus from our School of Church Music. Each of the 30-35 men was preparing for careers in music, which had been their college major. Now in graduate school, their abilities were far above mine. After working to crank up my nerve, I went to John Sims, the director of the chorus, and asked if I could sing with the group. I had to audition. After singing a bit for him, he looked up from the piano with a smile and said, "We will be glad to have a theolog in our group." I think he let me in because I was a theolog—student in the School of Theology. For the next two years I sang with the group, often feeling as if I was just making a joyful noise to the Lord when I compared myself to them. We would do a few guest performances, but mostly we just sang for seminary chapel worship. Essentially we were a church choir composed entirely of professionals, except for me. As far as I was concerned, the highlight of the experience was the rehearsals. On more than one occasion I was moved to tears by the sound, emotion, and feeling as we practiced. We were (I was) praising God and, with no human audience, only God was listening. There I learned the value of worship and praising God and God only, an audience of *One*.

Next we need to identify *where* we are to worship. The Psalmist said, "...in his sanctuary...in his mighty firmament!" (v.1) The usual interpretation of the sanctuary is a temple or a place deliberately prepared for the purpose of communal worship. The word can also mean the whole earth, which the Lord created and where God still is present. The firmament is interpreted to be all that is above the earth. It is a familiar concept to us from the Genesis story of creation. In the Psalm all heaven and earth are worthy places of worship. This fits the last verse of the Psalm that indicates anything that breathes is to praise God, both earthly and heavenly beings. For us it is important to remember the praise and worship of God cannot be limited to churches. It is perhaps more important in our age to understand that these are the specifically named places where worship should be located. It is not a case of choosing one or the other, but when we eliminate the special places created for this purpose we are likely to overlook the other possibilities.

Who is to praise the Lord is relatively easy to understand. As we have already indicated, it is everything that breathes. Elsewhere in the

Psalms (113:1) we are told the servants of the Lord are to praise Him. This is another way of describing the covenant people, the ones God has chosen, who are to praise Him. One purpose of this praising is for the nations of the world to see what the covenant people are doing and thereby be drawn into that same relationship. None are excluded from this call to worship. Let all the people praise God. A careful reading of the Psalm gives the impression that all the people have both the possibility and responsibility for praising God. The meaning is that anyone *can* praise God. Anyone *should* praise God.

The fourth aspect of our worship and praise of God can be identified by asking *when* can we do this? The first and last verses of Psalm 150 assume the process of praising God is continuous. It is a process that is enhanced and perpetuated by the regular observance of certain ritual and festive occasions. It may be weekly Sabbath, annual New Year, periodic harvest, or national celebrations. These occasions are important and help us perpetuate our faith or cultural values. More importantly, they help us maintain our own spiritual health. We can say we praise God continually, but we are usually deluding ourselves. We need regular appointed times to cultivate the attitude giving us the maturity and compulsion required for the continuous experiences we would like to possess. Experience has taught us that we have better health if we eat, sleep, and exercise at regular intervals and in regular places. This is also true with the practice of spiritual nourishment.

A fifth aspect of our praise and worship of God is opened when we ask, "*How* are we to do this?" Already we have identified places, persons, and times for this praise. The Psalmist surprises us with a long list of musical instruments which can be used in this praise. It seems as if he has read the scriptures carefully and listed every instrument they knew to be in his praise band. (vv.3-5) Then, he was very careful to include dance. (v.4) The Psalmist recognized what scientists and educators of today are discovering. The arts, and especially music, contribute to the educational development of the mature healthy mind and self. Verbal expressions in poetic form set to music can lift our emotions, increase our aspirations, and sharpen our visions beyond mere thought. The idea that we have to personally like every instrument or every song used to worship God would be foreign to the Psalmist. I don't think that either the Psalmist or Jesus would understand our present-day clashes over traditional or contemporary worship. They might be more inclined to remove church pews, put all our instruments—those we have and some we don't even know about—in one place and say, "Now, praise the Lord with song and dance."

Finally, the sixth aspect of praise found in the Psalms deals with the big question of *why?* We must not forget that the big reason is the sovereignty of God—the superiority of God over everything and everybody. This is covered by the phrase "according to his surpassing greatness." (v.2) We also praise God because of "his mighty deeds." (v.2) The Biblical words of forgiveness, redemption, salvation, deliverance, born again, and eternal life come to mind as we think of His deeds. Another way to explain it occurred as I was leaving church last Sunday. A variety of matters had occupied my time after morning worship, and I did not leave the building until about 3:00 p.m. No one else was here, and the parking lot was empty. As I walked toward my car on Willow Street, a young, nicely dressed man was approaching using the short-cut angle going toward Hyde Park Village. He was carrying a large handbag of some kind, probably for a computer and associated devices. It appeared to be made of very high quality leather. My little nylon bag stuffed full with books paled by comparison. We nodded to each other, and I slightly lifted my bag in his direction and said, "I'm glad yours is larger than mine, but I hope it is not so heavy." He responded, "You just came out of a place where they say if it's too heavy, He'll help you carry it." What profound insight he had about the result of worship and praise of God!! But we do it without expectation.

I'm sure you realize I was in that group of seminary students discussing the most important thing a person could do. I was not in the majority that night, but I was not alone in making the argument. More than four decades have passed since that memorable discussion. Well over two thousand years have passed since the Psalmist wrote the closing words to the Psalter. I believe he and I would have been on the same side of the debate. I also think Jesus would have agreed with our judgment. He learned much about the Father by singing these words. His example of prayer, worship, and praise indicate He learned the lessons well. Praise the Lord.

EPILOGUE

What can I do?
  I'm old.
    Bones are weak.
      Steps are slow.
        Voice is thin.
What can I do?
  Still it's my joyous chore to
    Praise God and
      Sing God's song.
Not circumstance nor time
  In this world or the next
    Can mute this song or
      Silence the praise.
What can I do?
  Continue to sing
    With dance, drums, threads,
      Paint, stone, and wood.
What can I do?
  Exhort you to join
    With glass, fiddles, horns,
      Flutes, sand and clay.
What can I do?
  Embrace the past.
    Push to the future.
      Hymn God again—and more!
I will do that.